Getting Started with Web Components

Build modular and reusable components using HTML, CSS and JavaScript

Prateek Jadhwani

BIRMINGHAM - MUMBAI

Getting Started with Web Components

Commissioning Editor: Pavan Ramchandani
Acquisition Editor: Pavan Ramchandani
Content Development Editor: Akhil Nair
Senior Editor: Hayden Edwards
Technical Editor: Jane Dsouza
Copy Editor: Safis Editing
Project Coordinator: Manthan Patel
Proofreader: Safis Editing
Indexer: Priyanka Dhadke
Production Designer: Arvindkumar Gupta

First published: August 2019
Production reference: 1080819

Published by Packt Publishing Ltd.
Livery Place
35 Livery Street
Birmingham
B3 2PB, UK.

ISBN 978-1-83864-923-4

www.packtpub.com

Packt>

packt.com

Subscribe to our online digital library for full access to over 7,000 books and videos, as well as industry leading tools to help you plan your personal development and advance your career. For more information, please visit our website

Why subscribe?

- Spend less time learning and more time coding with practical eBooks and Videos from over 4,000 industry professionals

- Improve your learning with Skill Plans built especially for you

- Get a free eBook or video every month

- Mapt is fully searchable

- Copy and paste, print, and bookmark content

Did you know that Packt offers eBook versions of every book published, with PDF and ePub files available? You can upgrade to the eBook version at www.packt.com and as a print book customer, you are entitled to a discount on the eBook copy. Get in touch with us at customercare@packtpub.com for more details.

At www.packt.com, you can also read a collection of free technical articles, sign up for a range of free newsletters, and receive exclusive discounts and offers on Packt books and eBooks.

Contributors

About the author

Prateek Jadhwani is a developer specializing in frontend technologies, living and working in the US. His experience includes 10 years of working as a frontend developer for many high-profile clients and many early-adoption side projects. Prateek had his first exposure to Web Components in 2014, and instantly fell in love with component-driven methodologies. Since then, he has evangelized Web Components and its related libraries to people at work and outside of work. Prateek loves all things open source and enjoys writing good JavaScript. A love for programming in general and a thirst for knowledge provide the motivation he carries through his work.

About the reviewer

Anchal Sarraf has 6 years of IT experience. She has worked on core automation development for the last 3 years with an IT multinational corporation. She is always eager to learn. She invests lots of her time in learning and teaching. Her aim is to make learning easy and exciting. She has also published a video tutorial course on UiPath on the online learning platform Udemy.

> *I would like to thank my parents and siblings for their constant support.*

Packt is searching for authors like you

If you're interested in becoming an author for Packt, please visit `authors.packtpub.com` and apply today. We have worked with thousands of developers and tech professionals, just like you, to help them share their insight with the global tech community. You can make a general application, apply for a specific hot topic that we are recruiting an author for, or submit your own idea.

Table of Contents

Preface

This book covers information about a web technology called Web Components. Web components are web specifications that provide the user with a component-driven methodology for development. It also provides encapsulation and allows you to use a component-driven methodology without any dependencies.

Who this book is for

This book is for developers who have heard about web components, but don't really know where to start. This book is also for intermediate and advanced developers who know what web components are, but are still afraid to use them in production. This book is also for frontend engineers who are simply looking into web components in order to increase their knowledge and skills.

You can also use this book to learn about and get into component-driven methodologies. If you are coming from a React/Angular/Polymer background, this book will give you an insight into how most things can be achieved using vanilla JavaScript without any libraries.

What this book covers

Chapter 1, *Web Components Essentials and Specifications*, discusses the concept of web components and the specifications associated with them.

Chapter 2, *Web Components Life Cycle Callback Methods*, covers various life cycle callback methods associated with web components.

Chapter 3, *Universal Web Components*, explores various concepts, such as styling and accessibility, that can increase the usability of web components.

Chapter 4, *Building Reusable Web Components*, explains the concept of reusability and looks into the concept of slots.

Chapter 5, *Managing States and Props*, discusses the concepts of states and props and how it can be achieved with the help of properties, attributes, and custom event handlers.

Chapter 6, *Building a Single Page App using Web Components*, looks into the process of creating a full-fledged single-page web app using just web components.

Chapter 7, *Implementing Web Components using Polymer and Stencil*, covers how different libraries and frameworks are different from vanilla web components.

Chapter 8, *Integrating Web Components with a Web Framework*, explores how we can integrate vanilla web components into existing projects with other libraries.

The book also contains a lot of examples—more than 50 web component examples—that can be referred to by both beginners and advanced users.

To get the most out of this book

To get the most out of this book, you need to comply with the following:

- You will need a basic understanding of web development technologies such as HTML, CSS, and JavaScript.
- You should be able to open websites on a browser and debug them using developer tools.
- You should be familiar with GitHub, since it has all the code files you'll need.
- You should be able to use Node.js (https://nodejs.org/en/) via Terminal or Command Prompt.
- You should be able to use a text editor.

Download the example code files

You can download the example code files for this book from your account at www.packt.com. If you purchased this book elsewhere, you can visit www.packt.com/support and register to have the files emailed directly to you.

You can download the code files by following these steps:

1. Log in or register at www.packt.com.
2. Select the **SUPPORT** tab.
3. Click on **Code Downloads & Errata**.
4. Enter the name of the book in the **Search** box and follow the onscreen instructions.

Once the file is downloaded, please make sure that you unzip or extract the folder using the latest version of:

- WinRAR/7-Zip for Windows
- Zipeg/iZip/UnRarX for Mac
- 7-Zip/PeaZip for Linux

The code bundle for the book is also hosted on GitHub at `https://github.com/PacktPublishing/Getting-Started-with-Web-Components`. In case there's an update to the code, it will be updated on the existing GitHub repository.

We also have other code bundles from our rich catalog of books and videos available at `https://github.com/PacktPublishing/`. Check them out!

Download the color images

We also provide a PDF file that has color images of the screenshots/diagrams used in this book. You can download it here: `https://static.packt-cdn.com/downloads/9781838649234_ColorImages.pdf`.

Conventions used

There are a number of text conventions used throughout this book.

`CodeInText`: Indicates code words in text, database table names, folder names, filenames, file extensions, path names, dummy URLs, user input, and Twitter handles. Here is an example: "A user looking for a music player with the ability to show liked or disliked songs will end up using the `<music-player>` component rather than something else."

A block of code is set as follows:

```
class myClass {
 constructor() {
 // do stuff
 }
}
```

When we wish to draw your attention to a particular part of a code block, the relevant lines or items are set in bold:

```
class HelloWorld extends HTMLElement {
  constructor() {
    super();

    // do magic here
    this.innerText = 'Hello World';
  }
}
```

Any command-line input or output is written as follows:

```
$ py -m http.server
```

Bold: Indicates a new term, an important word, or words that you see onscreen. For example, words in menus or dialog boxes appear in the text like this. Here is an example: "Enter your NPM package name and click on the **Publish** button."

Warnings or important notes appear like this.

Tips and tricks appear like this.

Get in touch

Feedback from our readers is always welcome.

General feedback: If you have questions about any aspect of this book, mention the book title in the subject of your message and email us at customercare@packtpub.com.

Errata: Although we have taken every care to ensure the accuracy of our content, mistakes do happen. If you have found a mistake in this book, we would be grateful if you would report this to us. Please visit www.packt.com/submit-errata, selecting your book, clicking on the Errata Submission Form link, and entering the details.

Piracy: If you come across any illegal copies of our works in any form on the Internet, we would be grateful if you would provide us with the location address or website name. Please contact us at copyright@packt.com with a link to the material.

If you are interested in becoming an author: If there is a topic that you have expertise in and you are interested in either writing or contributing to a book, please visit authors.packtpub.com.

Reviews

Please leave a review. Once you have read and used this book, why not leave a review on the site that you purchased it from? Potential readers can then see and use your unbiased opinion to make purchase decisions, we at Packt can understand what you think about our products, and our authors can see your feedback on their book. Thank you!

For more information about Packt, please visit packt.com.

Web Components Essentials and Specifications

Welcome to the world of Web Components.

Web Components, as the name indicates, are components that can be reused across different sections of a website by keeping encapsulation in check. They can even be published on the web, and be used by another site with the help of a simple import. This book covers all there is to know about Web Components. What they are made up of, how they can be used and in what scenarios. The book also covers wide variety of moderate and advanced level concepts such as good practices and integrating Web Components with other technologies.

In this chapter, we will talk about what Web Components are and how we can identify them while browsing various sites. We will also be talking about the specifications that make up Web Components along with detailed examples. You will be able to understand what custom elements are and how you can create one on your own. You will be able to encapsulate your Web Components with the help of a shadow DOM, and you will be able to use templates to achieve reusability.

While this chapter talks only about the basics of Web Components, by the end of this chapter you will be able to create your own Web Components from scratch, and understand the specifications associated with them.

In this chapter, we will cover the following topics:

- Web Components
- Web Component specifications

Technical requirements

In order to run the code, you will need a simple server, say a Python `SimpleHTTPServer`. In order to see the code on the browser, first start the server. On Mac, use the following command:

```
py -m SimpleHTTPServer
```

On Windows, use the following command in the folder that you have the code :

```
py -m http.server
```

and then you can simply go to `localhost:8080`. It will run `index.html` for you in that folder.

Web Components

Let's say you have a phone with a touchscreen. This touchscreen is a component of the mobile phone, working in conjunction with various other components, such as the circuit board and battery. Very few of us know how a phone screen works individually, yet we're all able to operate a mobile phone with ease. The same can be said of Web Components, which are the complex building blocks of websites which become navigable to all.

More importantly, the millions of phone screens around the world today are largely based on only a handful of designs. Fundamentally, the technology behind the mobile component is reusable and adaptable, and the same principle applies to Web Components.

The above points show how component methodology can be useful in creating a better product. Now, you must be thinking, why do we even need to look into the concept of components on the web? Well, I would like you to recall the last five sites that you visited. All these five sites probably shared a few features in common. Some of these are a header, a footer, some sort of menu, and an advertisement section. All these features, in terms of functionality, are doing the same thing. The only thing that differs is the look and feel.

Let us consider another use case where the site domain is the same but there are multiple web apps running on that domain.

We have all used Google or at least two or three Google services. If we observe, there is a section at the top-right corner on any of the Google services/sites. It's your account information, the one with your profile picture. And it shows the list of accounts you have logged in with:

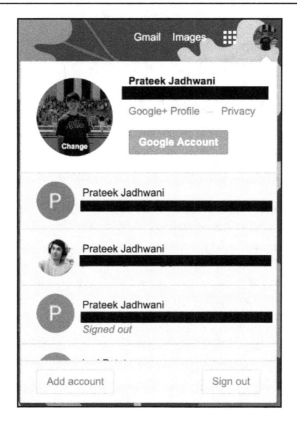

You will be able to see a similar account information card when you go from one service to another. Imagine being able to convert this functionality into an HTML tag `<account-info>` and being able to reuse it again and again on different services. This can be achieved with the help of Web Components.

A Web Component is a collection of specifications that lets a user create a functionality with a certain look and feel and which can be reused in such a way that all this functionality is encapsulated.

Just like the preceding example, `<account-info>`, a Web Component lets you put your functionality into its own custom name, which can be represented by an HTML tag, and then encapsulate its functionality. This encapsulation makes it easy to distribute and it can be reused again and again very easily.

In all, a Web Component lets you create a custom HTML tag that can be reused, and whose functionality is encapsulated from the user.

Now that we know what Web Components are and what Web Components can do, let's talk about Web Component specifications.

Web Component specifications

Just like any technology, Web Components also have a set of specifications that need to be followed in order to achieve the functionality associated with them.

A Web Component specification has the following parts:

- **Custom element**: The ability to create custom HTML tags and make sure that the browser understands how to use this HTML tag
- **Shadow DOM**: The ability to encapsulate the contents of the component from other parts of the DOM
- **Template**: Being able to create a reusable DOM structure that can be modified on the fly and output desired results

These three specifications, when used together, provide a way to create a custom HTML tag that can output desired results (DOM structure) and let it encapsulate from the page, making it reusable again and again.

Now that we know these specifications and what they do, let's dive into them individually and try to look at their JavaScript APIs.

Custom elements

A custom element specification lets you create a custom HTML tag that can be used as its own HTML tag on the page. In order to achieve this, we need to first write a class with the functionalities associated with that HTML element, and then we need to register it so that the browser understands what this HTML tag is, and how it can be used on the page.

If you are someone who is new to the concept of classes in JavaScript, here is how you can create a class:

```
class myClass {
  constructor() {
    // do stuff
  }
}
```

Pretty simple, right? Let's use the same class structure to create our custom element class, say `HelloWorld`:

```
class HelloWorld extends HTMLElement {
  constructor() {
    // very important
    // needed in every constructor
    // which extends another class
    super();

    // do magic here
    this.innerText = 'Hello World';
  }
}
```

In the preceding code, our custom element class is called `HelloWorld` and it is extending interface from the `HTMLElement` class, which represents how an HTML element should work on a page. So, `HelloWorld` now knows what click events are, what CSS is, and so on, simply by extending `HTMLElement`.

Inside this class, we have the `constructor()` method, which gets called as soon as a new instance of this class is created. The `super()` function needs to be called in order to correctly instantiate the properties of the extended class.

The preceding code simply creates the element class definition. We still need to register this element. We can do so by writing the following code:

```
customElements.define('hello-world', HelloWorld);
```

What it does is register the class `HelloWorld` by defining it using the `define()` interface in the `customElements` interface; `hello-world` is the name of the custom element that is going to be available on the page.

Once this is defined, you can used the custom element by simply writing the HTML tag as following:

```
<hello-world><hello-world>
```

When this code is run on a browser, it will render the text, **Hello World**.

 Final code: `https://codepen.io/prateekjadhwani/pen/jJZmyy`.

Types of custom elements

Now that you have understood how we can register custom elements, it is time we looked deeper into the type of custom elements. Based on the type of requirement, we can create two types of custom elements:

- **Autonomous custom element**: Any element that can be used by itself, without depending on another HTML element can be considered an autonomous custom element. In technical terms, Any custom hat extends `HTMLElement` is an autonomous custom element.

  Let's have another example of an autonomous custom element. Let's create a `SmileyEmoji` element that shows a smiley emoji. Here is what it looks like:

  ```
  class SmileyEmoji extends HTMLElement {
    constructor() {
      super();
      // let's set the inner text of
      // this element to a smiley
      this.innerText = '😃';
    }
  }

  customElements.define('smiley-emoji', SmileyEmoji);
  ```

  This registers the `smiley-emoji` custom element, which can be used as follows:

  ```
  <smiley-emoji></smiley-emoji>
  ```

- **Customized built-in element**: This type of custom element can extend the functionality of an already existing HTML tag. Let's create a custom element that extends `HTMLSpanElement` instead of `HTMLElement`. And its functionality is, say, it needs to add a smiley emoji at the end of the custom element:

  ```
  class AddSmiley extends HTMLSpanElement {
    constructor() {
      super();

      // lets append a smiley
      // to the inner text
      this.innerText += '😃';
    }
  }
  customElements.define('add-smiley', AddSmiley, { extends: 'span'
  });
  ```

Now, if you have the following HTML, this will add the smiley to the end of the text Hello World:

```
<span is="add-smiley">Hello World</span>
```

Final code: https://codepen.io/prateekjadhwani/pen/RdQarm.

Try running the code for autonomous custom elements and customized built-in elements on a browser, or CodePen, or JSFiddle. The class and registration code will be in the JavaScript block and the rest will be in the HTML block.

Notice the difference in registration code for <smiley-emoji> and <add-smiley> custom elements. The second one uses an extra parameter that specifies what it is extending.

You can check whether a custom element is already defined or not with the help of the following code:

```
customElements.get('smiley-emoji');
```

It will either return undefined if it has not been registered, or will return the class definition, if it has been registered. This is a very helpful statement in large projects because registering an already registered custom element will break the code.

Final code: https://codepen.io/prateekjadhwani/pen/moXPBd.

Shadow DOM

This is the second specification for Web Components and this one is responsible for encapsulation. Both the CSS and DOM can be encapsulated so that they are hidden from the rest of the page. What a shadow DOM does is let you create a new root node, called shadow root, that is hidden from the normal DOM of the page.

However, even before we jump into the concept of a shadow DOM, let's try to look at what a normal DOM looks like. Any page with a DOM follows a tree structure. Here I have the DOM structure of a very simple page:

```
▼ #document
    <!doctype html>
    <html lang="en" class=" -webkit-">
    ▼ <head>
        <title>Simple html page</title>
      </head>
    ▼ <body translate="no">
        <title>Understanding HTML Nodes</title>
        <h1>This is H1</h1>
        <p>This is p tag</p>
      </body>
    </html>
```

In the preceding image, you can see that `#document` is the root node for this page.

 You can find out the root node of a page by typing `document.querySelector('html').getRootNode()` in the browser console.

If you try to get the child nodes of an HTML tag using `document.querySelector('html').childNodes` in the browser console, then you can see the following screenshot:

```
▼ NodeList(3) [head, text, body]
  ▶ 0: head
  ▶ 1: text
  ▶ 2: body
    length: 3
  ▶ __proto__: NodeList
```

 Final code: `https://codepen.io/prateekjadhwani/pen/aMqBLa`.

This shows that the DOM follows a tree structure. You can go deeper into these nodes by clicking on the arrow right next to the name of the node. And just like how I have shown in the screenshot, anyone can go into a particular node by expanding it and change these values. In order to achieve this encapsulation, the concept of a shadow DOM was invented.

What a shadow DOM does is let you create a new root node, called shadow root, that is hidden from the normal DOM of the page. This shadow root can have any HTML inside and can work as any normal HTML DOM structure with events and CSS. But this shadow root can only be accessed by a shadow host attached to the DOM.

For example, let's say that instead of having text inside the <p> tag in the preceding example, we have a shadow host that is attached to a shadow root. This is what the page source would look like:

```
▼ #document
    <!doctype html>
    <html lang="en" class=" -webkit-">
    ▼ <head>
        <title>Simple html page with Shadow DOM</title>
      </head>
    ▼ <body translate="no">
        <title>Understanding HTML Nodes</title>
        <h1>This is H1</h1>
        ▼ <p>
          ▼ #shadow-root (open)
              <span>This is span tag</span>
          </p>
      </body>
    </html>
```

Furthermore, if you tried to get the child nodes of this <p> tag, you would see something like this:

```
>  document.querySelector('p').childNodes
<  ▼ NodeList []
        length: 0
      ▶ __proto__: NodeList
```

Notice that there is a <span> tag in the shadow root. Even though this <span> tag is present inside the <p> tag, the shadow root does not let JavaScript APIs touch it. This is how the shadow DOM encapsulates code inside itself.

Final code: `https://codepen.io/prateekjadhwani/pen/LaQxEY.`

Now that we know what a shadow DOM does, let's jump on to some code and learn how to create our own shadow DOMs.

Let's say we have a DOM with a class name entry. This is what it looks like:

```
<div class="entry"></div>
```

In order to create a shadow DOM in this `div`, we will first need to get the reference to this `.entry` div, then we need to mark it as a shadow root, and then append the content to this shadow root. So, here is the JavaScript code for creating a `shadowRoot` inside a `div` and adding contents to it:

```
// get the reference to the div
let shadowRootEl = document.querySelector('.entry');

// mark it as a shadow root
let shadowRoot = shadowRootEl.attachShadow({mode: 'open'});

// create a random span tag
// that can be appended to the shadow root
let childEl = document.createElement('span');
childEl.innerText = "Hello shadow DOM";

// append the span tag to shadow root
shadowRoot.appendChild(childEl);
```

Final code: `https://codepen.io/prateekjadhwani/pen/JzpWYE.`

Pretty simple, right? Remember, we are still discussing the shadow DOM spec. We haven't started implementing it inside a custom element yet. Let's recall the definition of our `hello-world` custom element. This is what it looked like:

```
class HelloWorld extends HTMLElement {
  constructor() {
    super();

    // do magic here
    this.innerText = 'Hello World';
```

```
    }
}

customElements.define('hello-world', HelloWorld);
```

Notice that the text `Hello World` is currently being added to normal DOM. We can use the same shadow DOM concepts discussed earlier in this custom element.

First, we need to get the reference to the node where we want to attach the shadow root. In this case, let's make the custom element itself the shadow host by using the following code:

```
let shadowRoot = this.attachShadow({mode: 'open'});
```

Now, we can either add a text node or create a new element and append it to this `shadowRoot`:

```
// add a text node
shadowRoot.append('Hello World');
```

 Final code: `https://codepen.io/prateekjadhwani/pen/LaQyPB`.

Templates

Till now, we have only created custom elements and shadow DOMs that require only one or, at the most, two lines of HTML code. If we move on to a real-life example, HTML code can be more than two lines. It can start from a few lines of nested `div` to images and paragraphs—you get the picture. The template specification provides a way to hold HTML on the browser without actually rendering it on the page. Let us look at a small example of a template:

```
<template id="my-template">
 <div class="red-border">
 <p>Hello Templates</p>
 <p>This is a small template</p>
 </div>
</template>
```

You can write a template inside `<template>` tags and assign it an identifier, just as I have done with the help of an `id`. You can put it anywhere on the page; it does not matter. We can get its content with the help of JavaScript APIs and then clone it and put it inside any DOM, just as I have shown in the following:

```
// Get the reference to the template
let templateReference = document.querySelector('#my-template');

// Get the content node
let templateContent = templateReference.content;

// clone the template content
// and append it to the target div
document.querySelector('#target')
    .appendChild(templateContent.cloneNode(true));
```

Similarly, we can have any number of templates on the page, which can be used by any JavaScript code.

 Final code: `https://codepen.io/prateekjadhwani/pen/ZPxOeq`.

Let's now use the same template with a shadow DOM. We will keep the template as it is. The changes in the JavaScript code would be something like this:

```
// Get the reference to the template
let templateReference = document.querySelector('#my-template');

// Get the content node
let templateContent = templateReference.content;

// Get the reference to target DOM
let targetDOM = document.querySelector('#target');

// add a shadow root to the target reference DOM
let targetShadowRoot = targetDOM.attachShadow({mode: 'open'});

// clone the template content
// and append it to the target div
targetShadowRoot.appendChild(templateContent.cloneNode(true));
```

We are doing the same thing that we did in the previous example, but, instead of appending the code directly to the target `div`, we are first attaching a shadow root to the target `div`, and then appending the cloned template content.

 Final code: `https://codepen.io/prateekjadhwani/pen/moxroz`.

We should be able to use the exact same concept inside the autonomous custom element that uses a shadow DOM. Let's give it a try.

Let's edit the `id` of the template and call it `hello-world-template`:

```
<template id="hello-world-template">
  <div>
    <p>Hello Templates</p>
    <p>This is a small template</p>
  </div>
</template>
```

We will follow the exact same approach that we followed in the preceding example. We will get the template content from the template reference, clone it, and append it in the custom element, making the code of the custom element look like the following:

```
class HelloWorld extends HTMLElement {
  constructor() {
    super();
    // Get the reference to the template
    let templateReference = document.querySelector('#hello-world-template');
    // Get the content node
    let templateContent = templateReference.content;

    let shadowRoot = this.attachShadow({mode: 'open'});
    // add a text node
    shadowRoot.append(templateContent.cloneNode(true));
  }
}

customElements.define('hello-world', HelloWorld);
```

Now we can simply call the HTML tag inside our page using the following code:

```
<hello-world></hello-world>
```

If we inspect the DOM structure inside developer tools, this is what we see:

```
▼<hello-world>
  ▼#shadow-root (open)
    ▼<div>
        <p>Hello Templates</p>
        <p>This is a small template</p>
      </div>
  </hello-world>
```

Final code: `https://codepen.io/prateekjadhwani/pen/ywKgBp.`

Module loader API

Module loader API is not a part of Web Component spec sheet, but it is definitely something that is useful to know when it comes to creating and using multiple classes. As the name says, this specification lets a user load the modules. That is, if you have a bunch of classes, you can use module loaders to load these classes into the web page.

If your build process involves using WebPack or Gulp or anything else that lets you import modules directly or indirectly, please feel free to skip this section.

Let's start with the basics. Let's say we have our `index.html` like this:

```
<!DOCTYPE html>
<html lang="en" dir="ltr">
  <head>
  </head>
  <body>
    <p>Placeholder for Random Number</p>
  </body>
</html>
```

We can see that there is a `<p>` tag in this HTML file. Now, let's say we have a class called `AddNumber`, whose purpose is to add a random number between 0 and 1 to this `<p>` tag. This would make the code look something like this:

```
<!DOCTYPE html>
<html lang="en" dir="ltr">
  <head>
  </head>
  <body>
    <p>Placeholder for Random Number</p>

    <script type="text/javascript">
      class AddNumber {
        constructor() {
          document.querySelector('p').innerText = Math.random();
        }
      }

      new AddNumber();
    </script>

  </body>
</html>
```

Simple, right? If you open the page on a browser, you will simply see a random number, and if you inspect the page, you will see that the random number replaced the text which was inside the `<p>` tag.

If we choose to store it in a JavaScript file, we can try to import it using the following code, where `addNumber.js` is the name of the file:

```
<script type="text/javascript" src="./addNumber.js"></script>
```

Now, let's say you have a `randomNumberGenerator` function instead of the `Math.random()` method. The code would look something like this:

```
class AddNumber {
  constructor() {
    // let's set the inner text of
    // this element to a smiley
    document.querySelector('p').innerText = randomNumberGenerator();
  }
}
function randomNumberGenerator() {
  return Math.random();
}
new AddNumber();
```

We also want the ability to let the user create a new object of the AddNumber class, rather than us creating it in the file. We do not want the user to know how randomNumberGenerator works, so we want the user to be only able to create the object of AddNumber. This way, we reach how modules work. We, the creators of modules, decide which functionalities the user can use and which they cannot.

We can choose what the user can use with the help of the export keyword. This would make the code look something like this:

```
//addNumber.js

export default class AddNumber {
  constructor() {
    document.querySelector('p').innerText = randomNumberGenerator();
  }
}

function randomNumberGenerator() {
  return Math.random();
}
```

When this file is imported (note that we haven't talked about imports yet), the user will only be able to use the AddNumber class. The randomNumberGenerator function won't be available to the user.

Similarly, if you have another file with, say, two other functions, add() and subtract(), you can export both of them as shown in the following:

```
// calc.js

export function add(x, y) {
  return x + y;
}

export function subtract(x, y) {
  return x - y;
}
```

Importing a module can be easily done with the help of the import keyword. In this section, we will talk about the type="module" attribute.

Inside the HTML file, `index.html`, instead of `type=text/javascript`, we can use `type=module` to tell the browser that the file that we are importing is a module. This is what it will look like when we are trying to import the file `addNumber.js`:

```
<script type="module" >
  import AddNumberWithNewName from './addNumber.js';
  new AddNumberWithNewName();
</script>
```

This is how it will look if we import functions from the `calc.js` module:

```
<script type="module" >
 import {add, subtract} from './calc.js';
 console.log(add(1,5));
</script>
```

Notice how we can change the name of the module exported from `AddNumber`, which uses `export default`, and how we have to use the same name as the name of the function exported using `export`.

Named export versus default export

In the previous examples, that is, `addNumber.js` and `calc.js`, we saw that there are two ways to export something: `export` and `export default`. The simplest way to understand it is as follows: when a file exports multiple things with different names and when these names cannot be changed after import, it is a named export, whereas, when we export only one thing from a module file and this name can be changed to anything after the import, it is a default export.

Custom elements using imports

Let's say we need to create a Web Component that does a very simple task of showing a heading and a paragraph inside it, and the name of the custom element should be `<revamped-paragraph>`. This is what the definition of this Web Component would look like:

```
//revampedParagraph.js

export default class RevampedParagraph extends HTMLElement {
  constructor() {
    super();

    // template ref and content
```

```
    let templateReference = document.querySelector('#revamped-paragraph-
template');
    let template = templateReference.content;

    // adding html from template
    this.append(template.cloneNode(true));
  }
}
```

Our `index.html` file, the file that imports this module, would look like this:

```
<!DOCTYPE html>
<html lang="en" dir="ltr">
  <head>
    <title>Revamped Paragraph</title>

    <!--
      Notice how we use type="module"
    -->
    <script type="module">
      // imports object from the module
      // and names it as RevampedParagraph
      // You can name it anything you want
      // since it is a default export
      import RevampedParagraph from './revampedParagraph.js';

      // We are now defining the custom element
      customElements.define('revamped-paragraph', RevampedParagraph);
    </script>

  </head>
  <body>

    <revamped-paragraph></revamped-paragraph>

    <!--
      Template for
      Revamped Paragraph
    -->
    <template id="revamped-paragraph-template">
      <h1>Revamped Paragraph</h1>
      <p>This is the default paragraph inside
      the revamped-paragraph element</p>
    </template>

  </body>
</html>
```

Notice how the template is a part of our HTML, and how it gets used when the module is imported. We will be learning about all the steps that take place from the actual registration of the Web Components to what happens when they are removed from the page in the next chapter, where we will learn about life cycle methods. But for now, we need to look at more examples to understand how to create Web Components.

Let's take a look at another example. In this example, we need to import multiple Web Components in the `index.html` file. The components are as follows:

- **A student attendance table component**: A table that shows the index number, student name, and attendance in a checkbox. This data is obtained from a `student.json` file.
- **An information banner component**: The purpose of this component is to show a phone number and an address for the school where these students are studying.
- **A time slot component**: A component that lets the user select a time slot for the class between three sets of timings.

Let us start with the first one, the `<student-attendance-table>` component. We need to first identify what it needs. In my opinion, these are the things it needs:

- A `fetch` call to the `student.json` file
- A template for each row of the string. I will be using template strings here
- A default text that says **loading...** when it is making the call and another text that says **unable to retrieve student list.** when the fetch call fails

This is what our `student.json` file looks like:

```
[
    {
      "name": "Robert De Niro",
      "lastScore": 75
    },
    {
      "name": "Jack Nicholson",
      "lastScore": 87
    },
    {
      "name": "Marlon Brando",
      "lastScore": 81
    },
    {
      "name": "Tom Hanks",
      "lastScore": 62
    },
```

```
    {
      "name": "Leonardo DiCaprio",
      "lastScore": 92
    }
  ]
```

This is what the definition of the Web Component looks like:

```
// StudentAttendanceTable.js

export default class StudentAttendanceTable extends HTMLElement {
  constructor() {
    super();

    // we simply called another method
    // inside the class
    this.render();
  }

  render() {
    // let put our loading text first
    this.innerText = this.getLoadingText();

    // let's start our fetch call
    this.getStudentList();
  }

  getStudentList() {
    // lets use fetch api
    // https://developer.mozilla.org/en-US/docs/Web
    // /API/Fetch_API/Using_Fetch
    fetch('./student.json')
    .then(response => {

      // converts response to json
      return response.json();

    })
    .then(jsonData => {
      this.generateTable(jsonData);
    })
    .catch(e => {

      // lets set the error message for
      // the user
      this.innerText = this.getErrorText();

      // lets print out the error
```

```
      // message for the devs
      console.log(e);
    });

  }

  generateTable(names) {
    // lets loop through names
    // with the help of map
    let rows = names.map((data, index) => {
      return this.getTableRow(index, data.name);
    });

    // creating the table
    let table = document.createElement('table');
    table.innerHTML = rows.join('');

    // setting the table as html for this component
    this.appendHTMLToShadowDOM(table);
  }

  getTableRow(index, name) {
    let tableRow = `<tr>
        <td>${index + 1}</td>
        <td>${name}</td>
        <td>
          <input type="checkbox" name="${index}-attendance"/>
        </td>
      </tr>`;

    return tableRow;
  }

  appendHTMLToShadowDOM(html) {
    // clearing out old html
    this.innerHTML = '';
    let shadowRoot = this.attachShadow({mode: 'open'});

    // add a text node
    shadowRoot.append(html);
  }

  getLoadingText() {
    return `loading..`;
  }

  getErrorText() {
    return `unable to retrieve student list.`;
```

```
    }
  }
```

Notice the functions `getLoadingText()` and `getErrorText()`. Their purpose is simply to return a text. Then the `render()` method first consumes the `getLoadingText()` method, and then makes the call using `getStudentList()` to fetch the student list from `student.json` file.

Once this student list is fetched, it gets passed onto `generateTable()` method, where every `name` and its `index` is passed into the `getTableRow()` method to generate rows and then gets returned back to be a part of the table. Once the table is formed, it is then passed into the `appendHTMLToShadowDOM()` method to be added to the shadow DOM for the component.

It's time to look into the `<information-banner>` component. Since this component simply needs to display a phone number and an address of the school where they are studying, we can use `<template>` and make it work. This is what it looks like:

```
//InformationBanner.js

export default class InformationBanner extends HTMLElement {
  constructor() {
    super();

    // we simply called another method
    // inside the class
    this.render();
  }

  render() {

    // Get the reference to the template
    let templateReference = document.querySelector('#information-banner-
template');

    // Get the content node
    let templateContent = templateReference.content;

    let shadowRoot = this.attachShadow({mode: 'open'});

    // add the template text to the shadow root
    shadowRoot.append(templateContent.cloneNode(true));
  }
}
```

Furthermore, `information-banner-template` looks something like this:

```
<template id="information-banner-template">
  <div>
    <a href="tel:1234567890">Call: 1234567890</a>
    <div>
      <p>Just Some Random Street</p>
      <p>Town</p>
      <p>State - 123456</p>
    </div>
  </div>
</template>
```

As you can see, it is not much different than the custom elements we have already talked about in previous sections.

Let's move on to the last custom element, the `<time-slot>` component. Since it also involves a preset number of time slots, we can use a `<template>` tag to do our work.

The template would look something like this:

```
<template id="time-slot-template">
  <div>
    <div>
      <input type="radio" name="timeslot" value="slot1" checked> 9:00
      AM - 11:00 AM
    </div>
    <div>
      <input type="radio" name="timeslot" value="slot2"> 11:00 AM -
      1:00 PM
    </div>
    <div>
      <input type="radio" name="timeslot" value="slot3"> 1:00 PM - 3:00
      PM
    </div>
  </div>
</template>
```

The definition of the `<time-slot>` component would look like this:

```
// TimeSlot.js

export default class TimeSlot extends HTMLElement {
  constructor() {
    super();

    // we simply called another method
    // inside the class
```

```
      this.render();
    }

    render() {

      // Get the reference to the template
      let templateReference = document.querySelector('#time-slot-
      template');

      // Get the content node
      let templateContent = templateReference.content;

      let shadowRoot = this.attachShadow({mode: 'open'});

      // add the template text to the shadow root
      shadowRoot.append(templateContent.cloneNode(true));
    }
  }
```

It is the same as the previous component.

Now that we have written the Web Components, it's time to take a look at the `index.html` file that includes all of these components together. This is what it looks like:

```
<!DOCTYPE html>
<html lang="en" dir="ltr">
  <head>
    <title>Student Page</title>

    <!--
      Notice how we use type="module"
    -->
    <script type="module">

      // importing the first custom element
      import StudentAttendanceTable from './StudentAttendanceTable.js';

      // importing the second custom element
      import InformationBanner from './InformationBanner.js';

      // importing the third custom element
      import TimeSlot from './TimeSlot.js';

      customElements.define('student-attendance-table',
      StudentAttendanceTable);
      customElements.define('information-banner', InformationBanner);
      customElements.define('time-slot', TimeSlot);
    </script>
```

```
  </head>
  <body>

    <time-slot></time-slot>
    <student-attendance-table></student-attendance-table>
    <information-banner></information-banner>

    <template id="information-banner-template">
      <div>
        <a href="tel:1234567890">Call: 1234567890</a>
        <div>
          <p>Just Some Random Street</p>
          <p>Town</p>
          <p>State - 123456</p>
        </div>
      </div>
    </template>

    <template id="time-slot-template">
      <div>
        <div>
          <input type="radio" name="timeslot" value="slot1" checked>
          9:00 AM - 11:00 AM
        </div>
        <div>
          <input type="radio" name="timeslot" value="slot2"> 11:00 AM -
          1:00 PM
        </div>
        <div>
          <input type="radio" name="timeslot" value="slot3"> 1:00 PM -
          3:00 PM
        </div>
      </div>
    </template>

  </body>
</html>
```

As you can see, one <script> tag of type="module" can import all three of them together, and can register the custom elements, which can be used in the <body> tag.

Summary

In this chapter, we talked about Web Components and how we are able to identify them in our daily web visits. We also talked about the specifications associated with Web Components, making it easier to understand even further. We looked into custom elements and how we can create our own custom elements. We talked about the shadow DOM and how it provides a level of encapsulation for our Web Components. We then talked about templates and how they provide an element of reusability inside a Web Component. We also looked into modules and how they let you create and add Web Components dynamically.

We dived deep into creating a Web Component with detailed code examples. With this, we should be able to create a simple Web Component from scratch without any issues.

In the next chapter, we will look into how we can make our Web Components do more with life cycle methods.

2

Web Components Life Cycle Callback Methods

In the last chapter, we talked about how to create a Web Component using vanilla JavaScript and HTML5. We discussed the specifications that are created in order to achieve the concept of Web Components. In this chapter, we will talk about life cycle events and the callback methods associated with them. A life cycle event is an event that occurs during the life cycle of a Web Component. This chapter deals with these events and how to access them with the help of callback methods.

In this chapter, we will cover the following topics:

- Overview of life cycle callback methods
- Life cycle callback methods currently available in Web Components

Overview of life cycle callback methods

Life cycle events are events that are triggered inside a web component when it reaches a certain stage of execution. These stages reflect the overall process of creating a web component and can be controlled with the help of life cycle callback methods. Life cycle callback methods are hooks or interfaces that get called back whenever a Web Component goes through these life cycle events.

Let me explain this with the help of an example. Suppose you have a shoe that you would like to wear. There may be certain events associated with the life cycle of this shoe. Let's say you want to wear it. You put your foot in and tie the lace. This triggers an event called `lacesTied()`. Now, you as a user who is wearing this shoe may choose to act on it. You can write a conditional block to check whether `lacesTiedStrength > 100` or whether `shoeSize < requiredShoeSize`. It depends on what you want to do. Similarly, there are life cycle callback methods associated with a Web Component that help the user capture certain execution states and write code effectively.

Types of life cycle callback methods

There are four life cycle callbacks available to Web Components as of now. These are as follows:

- connectedCallback()
- disconnectedCallback()
- adoptedCallback()
- attributeChangedCallback()

Let's discuss them in detail.

connectedCallback()

This interface/callback gets invoked every time a copy of a Web Component gets added to the DOM. This is very useful when it comes to initializing events associated with the DOM inside the component, or state management (see Chapter 5, *Managing States and Props*), or anything that needs any sort of initialization or pre-checks.

Let's take a look at an example. In Chapter 1, *Web Components Essentials and Specifications*, we talked about a <student-attendance-table> component, where the Web Component makes a fetch call to the file student.json, in order to retrieve the attendance data and then display that data in the form of a table.

The correct way to write that Web Component would be to add a connectedCallback() method to the definition of the StudentAttendenceTable class and then make the fetch call inside this callback.

This is what our code would look like:

```
// StudentAttendanceTable.js

export default class StudentAttendanceTable extends HTMLElement {
  constructor() {
    super();

    this.innerText = this.getLoadingText();
  }

  connectedCallback() {
    // let's start our fetch call
    this.getStudentList();
  }
```

```
getStudentList() {
  // lets use fetch api
  // https://developer.mozilla.org/en-US/docs/Web
  // /API/Fetch_API/Using_Fetch
  fetch('./student.json')
  .then(response => {

    // converts response to json
    return response.json();

  })
  .then(jsonData => {
    this.generateTable(jsonData);
  })
  .catch(e => {

    // lets set the error message for
    // the user
    this.innerText = this.getErrorText();

    // lets print out the error
    // message for the devs
    console.log(e);
  });

}

generateTable(names) {
  // lets loop through names
  // with the help of map
  let rows = names.map((data, index) => {
    return this.getTableRow(index, data.name);
  });

  // creating the table
  let table = document.createElement('table');
  table.innerHTML = rows.join('');

  // setting the table as html for this component
  this.appendHTMLToShadowDOM(table);
}

getTableRow(index, name) {
  let tableRow = `<tr>
      <td>${index + 1}</td>
      <td>${name}</td>
      <td>
        <input type="checkbox" name="${index}-attendance"/>
```

```
        </td>
      </tr>`;

    return tableRow;
  }

  appendHTMLToShadowDOM(html) {
    // clearing out old html
    this.innerHTML = '';

    let shadowRoot = this.attachShadow({mode: 'open'});

    // add a text node
    shadowRoot.append(html);
  }

  getLoadingText() {
    return `loading..`;
  }

  getErrorText() {
    return `unable to retrieve student list.`;
  }
}
```

As you can see in the code, we are now making a call to fetch the student list inside the connectedCallback() method. This makes sure that the code gets executed, once the Web Component is attached to the web page.

Another example of a place where using the connectedCallback is helpful is event handling. Let's say we have a Web Component that shows a custom button. And the purpose of this button is to show some text right next to it stating the number of times the button was clicked. If we try to use it without connectedCallback, it would look something like this:

```
// CustomButton.js

export default class CustomButton extends HTMLElement {
  constructor() {
    super();

    // Initializing an initial state
    this.timesClicked = 0;

    let template = `
      <button>Click Me</button>
      <span>${this.getTimesClicked()}</span>
```

```
      `;

    this.innerHTML = template;
  }

  connectedCallback() {

    // adding event handler to the button
    this.querySelector('button')
      .addEventListener('click', (e) => {
        this.handleClick(e);
      });
  }

  handleClick() {
    // updating the state
    this.timesClicked++;

    this.querySelector('span')
      .innerText = this.getTimesClicked();
  }

  getTimesClicked() {
    return `Times Clicked: ${this.timesClicked}`;
  }
}
```

The associated HTML would look like this:

```
<!DOCTYPE html>
<html lang="en" dir="ltr">
  <head>
    <title>Connected Callback Example</title>

    <!--
      Notice how we use type="module"
    -->
    <script type="module">

      /// importing the first custom element
      import CustomButton from './CustomButton.js';

      customElements.define('custom-button', CustomButton);
    </script>

  </head>
  <body>
```

```
            <custom-button></custom-button>

        </body>
    </html>
```

Notice how an event listener is bound to the DOM in the connectedCallback() method. We will be talking about event listeners in detail in the Chapter 5, *Managing States and Props*, but for now; we can use the code as an example. The preceding code makes sure that we bind a click event to the button only after the DOM is available on the page. This prevents us from creating event-related bugs, which I am sure has happened to every one of us.

disconnectedCallback()

Just like there are certain operations that need to be performed when a Web Component is added to the DOM, there are certain operations that need to be performed after the component is removed from the DOM. The most common example of this scenario is, again, event handlers. Event handlers consume memory, and, when the DOM associated with them is removed, the event handler is still on the page, listening to events, still consuming memory. The callback, disconnectedCallback(), gives Web Components a way to write code that can handle these scenarios.

Let's take a look at the <custom-button> element and how we can use disconnectedCallback() to remove the attached event:

```
// CustomButton.js

export default class CustomButton extends HTMLElement {
  constructor() {
    super();

    // Initializing an initial state
    this.timesClicked = 0;

    let template = `
      <button>Click Me</button>
      <span>${this.getTimesClicked()}</span>
    `;

    this.innerHTML = template;
  }

  connectedCallback() {
```

```
    // adding event handler to the button
    this.querySelector('button')
      .addEventListener('click', this.handleClick.bind(this));
  }

  disconnectedCallback() {
    console.log('We are inside disconnectedCallback');
    // adding event handler to the button
    this.querySelector('button')
      .removeEventListener('click', this.handleClick);
  }

  handleClick() {
    // updating the state
    this.timesClicked++;

    this.querySelector('span')
      .innerText = this.getTimesClicked();
  }

  getTimesClicked() {
    return `Times Clicked: ${this.timesClicked}`;
  }
}
```

If you look at the `disconnectedCallback()` method, we have a `console.log` statement and the code to remove the event. When you are running this Web Component on a page, you can manually remove the component and see that `disconnectedCallback()` gets called automatically. I prefer going to the **dev** console and typing the following code to see it happen:

```
document.querySelector('custom-button').remove();
```

This will remove the first instance of `<custom-button>` from the page, thus triggering the `disconnectedCallback()` method.

Removing an event handler is only one of the uses. There can be *any* number of use cases that need to be performed before removing the Web Component from the DOM.

adoptedCallback()

This callback gets triggered when the Web Component is moved from one parent to another.

Just like we had `connectedCallback` and `disconnectedCallback`, we can write `adoptedCallback` in the following way:

```
adoptedCallback() {
  console.log('I am adopted');
}
```

attributeChangedCallback()

Since all the custom elements act and behave like any other HTML element, they also have the ability to have attributes inside them. We will be discussing attributes in the coming chapter, but, for now, let's assume we have a custom element named `<my-name>`, whose purpose is to display the text **Hello, my name is John Doe**.

So, the definition of this Web Component would become something like this:

```
// MyName.js

export default class MyName extends HTMLElement {
  constructor() {
    super();

    this.innerText = 'Hello, my name is John Doe';
  }
}
```

Now, let's say we want to have a different name. And for every different name, we will need to have a different definition of the custom element, making a totally different Web Component. In order to fix this problem, we can use attributes. We can pass the name in an attribute inside the HTML tag of this element, making it look like this:

```
<my-name fullname="John Doe"></my-name>
```

But, in order to make a Web Component use the attributes provided, we will first ask it to observe certain attributes, which we can provide in an array like this:

```
static get observedAttributes() {
  return ['fullname'];
}
```

Here, we are just going to observe `fullname`. You can add more as per your requirement. We will be diving into attributes in the coming chapters.

Once we have started observing these attributes, we can then use the `attributeChangedCallback()` to make necessary changes to custom elements as per the requirement. I am simply updating the name in the following callback:

```
attributeChangedCallback(name, oldValue, newValue) {
  if (name == 'fullname') {
    this.innerText = 'Hello, my name is ' + newValue;
  }
}
```

As you can see, `attributeChangedCallback()` takes in three parameters: `name`, which is the name of the attribute changed, and `oldValue` and `newValue`, which are the values before and after the change, respectively.

In the preceding code, we are simply checking whether the name of the attribute is `fullname` and updating the text to say the updated name.

The full component code looks like this:

```
// MyName.js

export default class MyName extends HTMLElement {
  constructor() {
    super();

    this.innerText = 'Hello, my name is NO NAME';
  }

  static get observedAttributes() {
    return ['fullname'];
  }

  attributeChangedCallback(name, oldValue, newValue) {
    if (name == 'fullname') {
      this.innerText = 'Hello, my name is ' + newValue;
    }
  }
}
```

The `index.html` file associated with it becomes as follows:

```
<!DOCTYPE html>
<html lang="en" dir="ltr">
  <head>
    <title>Attribute Changed Callback Example</title>

    <!--
      Notice how we use type="module"
    -->
    <script type="module">

      /// importing the first custom element
      import MyName from './MyName.js';

      customElements.define('my-name', MyName);
    </script>

  </head>
  <body>

    <my-name fullname="John Doe"></my-name>

  </body>
</html>
```

As you can see, we are not doing anything different than what we have done in the previous sections.

Summary

In this chapter, we talked about what life cycle callback methods are and what purpose they serve. We talked about `connectedCallback()`, `disconnectedCallback()`, `adoptedCallback()`, and `attributeChangedCallback()`. We looked into various examples of how to use these callbacks and their practical uses.

In the next chapter, we will look into styling our Web Components with the help of CSS, and then we will talk about the gold standard checklist and its purpose.

Universal Web Components

3

In the last chapter, we talked about the various life cycle callback methods of Web Components. In this chapter, we will look into the styling of Web Components, with a lot of examples. Styling plays a vital role in the look and feel of a Web Component. We will also be taking a look at what accessibility does to our Web Components and understand the meaning of the Gold Standard Checklist and how this Gold Standard Checklist makes a Web Component extremely usable.

In this chapter, we will cover the following topics:

- Styling Web Components
- Accessibility for Web Components
- Gold Standard Checklist

Styling Web Components

In the previous chapters, we looked at custom elements that use a shadow DOM for encapsulation and custom elements that do not use a shadow DOM. We will be styling our Web Component for both of these types.

Let's say, we have a Web Component called `<company-header>`. For the sake of simplicity, this header component needs to have an icon on the left-hand side with a circular border and this icon needs to be a link; the name of the page should be right next to the icon, and then there should be two other links on the extreme right-hand side, say **home** and **about us**.

This is how it should be used inside the `index.html` file:

```
<company-header
    icon="icon.png"
     page-name="My Page">
</company-header>
```

If you are being a little bit adventurous, I would like you to stop reading for a while and write the completed code for this component based on the knowledge you have achieved in the previous chapters. Once you have done so, feel free to continue reading.

Now, based on the information provided as a requirement for the component, our `index.html` file would look something like this:

```
<!DOCTYPE html>
<html lang="en" dir="ltr">
  <head>
    <title>Custom header</title>

    <!--
      Notice how we use type="module"
    -->
    <script type="module">

      import CompanyHeader from './CompanyHeader.js';

      // We are now defining the custom element
      customElements.define('company-header', CompanyHeader);
    </script>

  </head>
  <body>

    <company-header
        icon="icon.png"
        page-name="My Page">
    </company-header>
  </body>
</html>
```

As you can see, we have done nothing different other than the way we are calling the `<company-header>` component. Let's take a look at the `CompanyHeader.js` file. Note that we are going to use the Web Component without a shadow DOM in this example:

```js
// CompanyHeader.js

export default class CompanyHeader extends HTMLElement {
  constructor() {

    // We are not even going to touch this.
    super();

    // Lets provide a default icon
    this.icon = 'newicon.jpeg';

    // Then lets render the template
    this.render();
  }

  render() {
    this.innerHTML = this.getTemplate();
  }

  // Lets get icon and page-name from attributes
  static get observedAttributes() {
    return ['icon', 'page-name'];
  }

  attributeChangedCallback(name, oldValue, newValue) {
    if (name == 'icon') {
      this.icon = newValue;
    }

    if (name == 'page-name') {
      this.pageName = newValue;
    }

    // Lets re-render after getting the new attributes
    this.render();
  }

  getTemplate() {
    return `
      <a href="/">
        <img class="icon" src="${this.icon}" />
      </a>
      <h1 class="heading">${this.pageName}</h1>
      <div>
```

```
            <a class="header-links" href="/home.html">Home</a>
            <a class="header-links" href="/aboutus.html">About Us</a>
          </div>
        `;
      }
    }
```

The `constructor()` interface is responsible for making sure that `icon` is set to a default file and the component renders properly without any issue. We also learned in the previous section about `attributeChangedCallback()`, so `get observedAttributes()` is simply creating a list of attributes to listen to for changes.

Furthermore `attributeChangedCallback()` is making sure that the changed attribute values are being used properly. The `getTemplate()` method simply returns an ES6 template string, which can be set as `innerHTML` of the Web Component.

Now that our Web Component is working fine, let's add the style for this component. Inside the `index.html` file, we can create a `<style>` tag and add our styles inside it:

```
<style>
  company-header {
    display: flex;
    background: #44afdc;
    align-items: center;
    padding: 0 10px;
  }
  .icon {
    width: 50px;
    height: 50px;
    border-radius: 50%;
  }
  .heading {
    flex: 1;
    color: white;
    padding-left: 20px;
  }
  .header-links {
    text-decoration: none;
    padding: 20px;
    color: white;
  }
</style>
```

This way, we can have the style attached directly to the `<company-header>` element.

However, now we may have a problem. There might be some other `div` with the class name `.heading`, and this CSS might bleed out to that other class. You may argue that we should namespace our CSS by adding `company-header` in front of the CSS used, making it look like the following:

```
<style>
  company-header {
    display: flex;
    background: #44afdc;
    align-items: center;
    padding: 0 10px;
  }
  company-header .icon {
    width: 50px;
    height: 50px;
    border-radius: 50%;
  }
  company-header .heading {
    flex: 1;
    color: white;
    padding-left: 20px;
  }
  company-header .header-links {
    text-decoration: none;
    padding: 20px;
    color: white;
  }
</style>
```

This may fix the problem a little bit, but does not fix it completely. It still doesn't fix the part where the `.heading` class CSS bleeds out to the `.heading` class in `company-header` and then gets overwritten by the `company-header` namespaced heading class. Hence, comes our shadow DOM specification.

Let us try to write the Web Component with a shadow DOM:

```
// CompanyHeader.js

export default class CompanyHeader extends HTMLElement {
  constructor() {

    // We are not even going to touch this.
    super();

    // Lets provide a default icon
    this.icon = 'newicon.jpeg';
```

```
    // lets create our shadow root
    this.shadowObj = this.attachShadow({mode: 'open'});

    // Then lets render the template
    this.render();
  }

  render() {

    this.shadowObj.innerHTML = this.getTemplate();
  }

  // Lets get icon and page-name from attributes
  static get observedAttributes() {
    return ['icon', 'page-name'];
  }

  attributeChangedCallback(name, oldValue, newValue) {
    if (name == 'icon') {
      this.icon = newValue;
    }

    if (name == 'page-name') {
      this.pageName = newValue;
    }

    // Lets re-render after getting the new attributes
    this.render();
  }

  getTemplate() {
    return `
      <a href="/">
        <img class="icon" src="${this.icon}" />
      </a>
      <h1 class="heading">${this.pageName}</h1>
      <div>
        <a class="header-links" href="/home.html">Home</a>
        <a class="header-links" href="/aboutus.html">About Us</a>
      </div>
    `;
  }
}
```

As you can see, most of the code is the same, other than the part where we create a shadow root and add our HTML inside this shadow root.

If you run the code now, you will see that our styles do not apply inside the Web Component. So, the CSS is not bleeding anymore. But, in order to get back our CSS, we will need to add it as the part of the template, making it look like this:

```
getTemplate() {
    return `
      <a href="/">
        <img class="icon" src="${this.icon}" />
      </a>
      <h1 class="heading">${this.pageName}</h1>
      <div>
        <a class="header-links" href="/home.html">Home</a>
        <a class="header-links" href="/aboutus.html">About Us</a>
      </div>
      <style>
        :host {
          display: flex;
          background: #44afdc;
          align-items: center;
          padding: 0 10px;
        }
        .icon {
          width: 50px;
          height: 50px;
          border-radius: 50%;
        }
        .heading {
          flex: 1;
          color: white;
          padding-left: 20px;
        }
        .header-links {
          text-decoration: none;
          padding: 20px;
          color: white;
        }
      </style>
    `;
}
```

Now, our component looks beautiful with all the CSS, but what is :host ?

While we can add CSS inside the shadow root with the help of selectors, we do not have a selector associated with the shadow root itself, which acts as a container for the HTML. So, we can have CSS attached to this shadow root with the help of the :host selector.

Let's try another example with styling. Let's say we have a requirement to design a Web Component that lets you log in with the help of a login form. It needs to have a bluish background, and when the login is successful, it should turn this background to a greenish shade. Also, for the sake of simplicity, the username-password check will simply perform a `Math.random()` operation and, if this value is greater than *0.5*, then the login is successful:

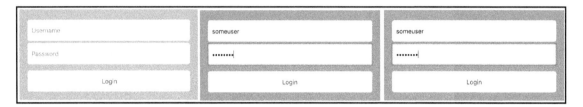

Let's jump into the code. There are no changes to our `index.html` other than us including this new component:

```
<script type="module">

  import CompanyLogin from './CompanyLogin.js';

  // We are now defining the custom element
  customElements.define('company-login', CompanyLogin);
</script>
```

The definition of this `CompanyLogin` class is shown in the preceding code.

Let's take a look at our HTML template. We want a username text field, a password text field, and a button that can be clicked:

```
getTemplate() {
  return `
    <input type="text" name="username" placeholder="Username"/>
    <input type="password" name="password" placeholder="Password"/>
    <button type="submit" class="login-button">Login</button>
  `;
}
```

Then we need to add this template HTML to our shadow root:

```
// lets create our shadow root
this.shadowObj = this.attachShadow({mode: 'open'});

this.shadowObj.innerHTML = this.getTemplate();
```

We also need a way to notify our Web Component as to when the button is being clicked:

```
connectedCallback() {
  this.shadowObj.querySelector('button')
    .addEventListener('click', (e) => this.handleLogin(e));
}
```

We chose `connectedCallback()` for event handling here since we need to bind events only when HTML is on the page. We can handle our click event inside the `handleLogin()` method:

```
handleLogin(e) {
  this.username = this.shadowObj.querySelector('[name=username]').value;
  this.password = this.shadowObj.querySelector('[name=password]').value;

  // Do what ever you want with these values
  console.log(this.username, this.password);

  // We will do things as per our requirement
  let loginSuccess = Math.random();
  if(loginSuccess > 0.5) {
    this.classList.add('login-success');
  } else {
    this.classList.add('login-failure');
  }
}
```

As you can see, we are simply printing the values of username and password. I chose to add a print example so that you have an idea about how it is very easy to read these values. We are also changing the class name of the actual Web Component based on the `Math.random()` function.

Now that we have a working component, we can start working on the CSS. We can add our CSS inside our template:

```
<style>
  :host {
    background: #68afe8;
    padding: 20px;
    display: flex;
    flex-direction: column;
    width: 400px;
    margin: 0 auto;
  }
  :host(.login-failure) {
    background: #f35353;
  }
```

```
  :host(.login-success) {
    background: #499c19;
  }
  input {
    margin-top: 5px;
    padding: 10px;
    height: 30px;
    font-size: 15px;
    border: none;
    border-radius: 5px;
  }
  button {
    margin-top: 15px;
    padding: 10px;
    font-size: 15px;
    border: none;
    height: 50px;
    border-radius: 5px;
    cursor: pointer;
  }
</style>
```

We are again using the `:host` selector as a way to add CSS to the shadow root of our Web Component. In the `handleLogin()` function, we are adding CSS classes to our Web Component. We can target those classes from inside our CSS by using `:host(<selector>)` just like we used it in the preceding code.

When we run our Web Component on a browser, it looks like this:

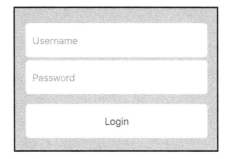

Based on the `random()` function, we can get either a greenish background, indicating that it is a successful login, or the one with a red background.

Accessibility for Web Components

Accessibility plays a vital role in web development. Our users can be limited to a keyboard, they might be using a screen reader, or could be color-blind. Making sure that our users are comfortable in all scenarios is the key to making a good site. Similarly, creating a good Web Component also includes making a Web Component accessible.

When you are creating a Web Component, you need to make sure that your Web Components are accessible at least up to a certain extent. For example, an image should always have `alt` text. A link should always have `alt` text. Input fields should have proper aria-labels. There should be sufficient color contrasts. Tab orders should be in the correct order, and so on.

Now that we know what can be done to make a component accessible, let's take a look at a small example. Let's say the requirement is to create a `<header-image>` component that shows a full-width image. In order to make sure that this component is accessible, the image used should have `alt` text.

Let's take a look at our `getTemplate()` function for this component:

```
getTemplate() {
  return `
    <img src="${this.getAttribute('src')}"
         alt="${this.getAttribute('alt')}"/>
    ${this.handleErrors()}
    <style>
      img {
        width: 400px;;
      }
    </style>
  `;
}
```

Here, we are adding an `alt` attribute to the image tag, and we are grabbing this `alt` text from the Web Component itself:

```
<header-image alt="Blue Clouds"
      src="clouds-sky-header.jpg">
</header-image>
```

We also have an error handler function called `handleErrors()`, which makes sure to tell the user that the component is missing `alt` text:

```
handleErrors() {
  if(!this.getAttribute('alt')) {
    return `
      <div class="error">Missing Alt Text</div>
      <style>
        .error {
          color: red;
        }
      </style>
    `;
  }

  return ``;
}
```

This will show a **Missing Alt Text** error message in red, when the component is missing the alt text. We can solve other accessibility issues in the same way.

Gold Standard Checklist

We have been creating Web Components in the previous sections, but, other than the accessibility, no other sections tell us what defines a good component. So, let's talk about it. The Gold Standard Checklist is a working draft (see `https://github.com/webcomponents/gold-standard/wiki`) that tells the creators of a Web Component what things should be taken care of in order to create a good, reusable component.

Let's talk about some of the points that I personally feel are important:

- Web components should be accessible. In order to make the Web Components work on all screens, we need to make sure that the component covers all aspects of accessibility.
- Binding of events should be done in `connectedCallback()`. This makes sure that the DOM to which events are bound will always be present, thus reducing the number of bugs.
- Event bindings should be removed in `disconnectedCallback()`, thus freeing up the memory that is not required anymore.

- Components should have default styling with good contrasting colors. This will make sure that components can be seen properly at all times.
- Components should also follow responsive designs. In order to make our component work on all screen sizes without any layout issues, we should make sure that we have responsive CSS associated with the Web Component.
- Components should be able to expose events. We will be talking about events in `Chapter 5`, *Managing States and Props*, but the main takeaway from this point is that, if you are building a component that needs to tell other components the change in state, it should tell them by exposing an event callback.

Even though the Gold Standard Checklist contains a lot of very good points, I feel that these six points should be able to make a component pretty good in terms of reusability. In case you are curious about the other points, here is the link to the full Gold Standard Checklist: `https://github.com/webcomponents/gold-standard/wiki`.

Summary

In this chapter, we looked into different ways we can style a Web Component, learned about accessibility and how it can be used in creating a more complete Web Component, and then looked into the Gold Standard Checklist, which provides guidelines for creating a good Web Component.

In the next chapter, we will be looking into reusability and how it can used in Web Components, along with how these Web Components are published on the web for maximum reusability.

4
Building Reusable Web Components

In the previous chapter, we talked about styling our Web Components, along with understanding how accessibility plays a vital role in creating a good component. We then talked about the Gold Standard Checklist and looked into unit testing.

In this chapter, we will be looking deep into reusability and how we can publish our Web Components on a platform for maximum reusability. We will also cover a few examples on responsive Web Components. We did look into styling, and while the concept of responsive CSS is not something new, the use of responsive styles could make a component look even better and more reusable.

In this chapter, we will cover the following topics:

- The concept of reusability
- Responsive Web Components
- Publishing Web Components
- Extending Web Components - slots

The concept of reusability

Before we even dive into the concept of reusability in Web Components, let's take a look at what reusability is with the help of an example. Let's take an example of an operating system, say Windows 10. Now, we all know there are a lot of computers. Some with the same hardware and some with different. But what makes this piece of software (Windows 10) reusable is its ability to being used again and again and in different scenarios without any issues. The exact same thing can be made to work for a Web Component.

Yes, Web Components can be made extremely reusable. Let's say we have a Web Component `<custom-header>`. As the name indicates, it is a header. And most of the sites that we have ever visited have one or the other version of the same functional header. The functionalities are as follows:

1. Show the logo.
2. Clicking on the logo should drop the user to `index.html`.
3. Show the name of the company.
4. Show user stats, that is, if the user is not logged in, show the login drop-down menu. If the user is logged in, show account-related links.
5. Show **Help** links.
6. Show **About us and Contact us** links.
7. Provide a default background for the header.
8. The header can be sticky at the top.

These points all show us various ways a header can be customized and implemented. We can very well convert these points to an attribute list while designing the Web Component:

```
<custom-header
  logo-url="icon.png"
  logo-alt-text="Company X logo"
  company-name-text="Company X"
  is-logged-in="user23411"
  help-link="/help.html"
  help-link-text="Help and Support"
  contact-us-link="/contact.html"
  contact-us-alt-text="Contact Us"
  background-color="#000000"
  text-color="#ffffff"
  is-sticky="true">
</custom-header>
```

Or if the user is not logged in, it can be left empty like this:

```
<custom-header
  logo-url="icon.png"
  logo-alt-text="Company X logo"
  company-name-text="Company X"
  is-logged-in=""
  help-link="/help.html"
  help-link-text="Help and Support"
  contact-us-link="/contact.html"
  contact-us-alt-text="Contact Us"
  background-color="#000000"
  text-color="#ffffff"
```

```
    is-sticky="true">
</custom-header>
```

All these attributes make the Web Component extremely reusable. The person who is going to use this component will simply need to import it and provide the values of these attributes without coding anything extra.

Let's take a look at another, but complex, example. Let us say you are building a music player. A Web Component `<music-player>` may have a bunch of attributes that make it extremely reusable. The common ones are as follows:

- Name of the song
- URL of the song
- Player color/contrast options
- Is playing, to tell whether the player is playing or not
- Play on load, to tell whether the player should start playing as soon as the player loads
- Show or hide playlist

And the uncommon ones could be as follows:

- Player size could be set to large, medium, or small
- Bottom sticky or top sticky, just like `Soundcloud` does
- Like or dislike song

Knowing these attributes and being able to implement them plays a very important role in creating a reusable component. A user looking for a music player with the ability to show liked or disliked songs will end up using the above-mentioned `<music-player>` component rather than something else.

The concept of reusability can be and should be applied to all the Web Components. It not only allows the Web Component to be used in more scenarios, it also makes it more maintainable, since we are making sure that it works in more scenarios.

Responsive Web Components

In the last chapter, we talked about adding styles to our Web Component to make it look beautiful. This time, we will take a look at it from a reusability perspective. What if a person who is trying to reuse our Web Component decides to use it in an inline tag, or what if the Web Component is used as a full-width component? Let us look into how our Web Component would be displayed inside different box models and how it would look on different screen sizes.

Building <profile-info> Web Component

Let us take a look at an example Web Component. Let's say we have a Web Component called <profile-info>. And the purpose of this Web Component is to show information about an employee. The information could be name, designation, ID number, profile picture, and a card background color to state whether the employee is a full-time employee, a part-time employee, or a contractor.

The HTML structure for this <profile-info> component would look something like this:

```
<profile-info
  name="John Doe"
  designation="Frontend Engineer - Marketing"
  id-number="PRC-1455"
  picture-src="./john-doe.png"
  employee-type="ft">
</profile-info>
```

From the list of attributes, we can see that it needs a name, designation, ID number, picture link, and employee type. This is what it needs to do in terms of functionality. In terms of look and feel, it needs to look like a card with rounded profile picture, along with all the remaining information. And based on the resolution of the screen, it needs be either full-width, or if the screen is that of a mobile device, it should be shown in the form of a card.

Let's do a mobile first approach on the Web Component, and start writing the code:

```
export default class ProfileInfo extends HTMLElement {
  constructor() {

    // We are not even going to touch this.
    super();

    // lets create our shadow root
    this.shadowObj = this.attachShadow({mode: 'open'});
```

```
    // Then lets render the template
    this.render();
  }

  render() {
    this.shadowObj.innerHTML = this.getTemplate();
  }

  getTemplate() {
    // Show HTML Here
  }
}
```

This is the most basic part that we have covered in the previous chapters. We are simply creating the component skeleton and making sure that the HTML for the shadow DOM is retrieved from the getTemplate() method.

For the mobile view, the card should look something like this:

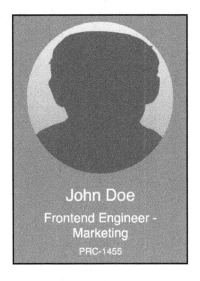

The HTML structure would look something like this:

```
getTemplate() {
  return `
    <div class="profile-info__container">
      <img class="profile-info__picture"
        src="${this.getAttribute('picture-src')}" />
      <div class="profile-info__text">
        <div class="profile-info__name">
          ${this.getAttribute('name')}
```

```
        </div>
        <div class="profile-info__designation">
          ${this.getAttribute('designation')}
        </div>
        <div class="profile-info__id-number">
          ${this.getAttribute('id-number')}
        </div>
      </div>
    </div>
    `;
}
```

If you take a look at the class names, they are all using BEM patterns.

 If you have no idea as to what BEM is, the full form of BEM is Block Element Modifier. It is a methodology of using logical and reusable CSS classes for modular HTML blocks. If you would like to look into it, feel free to look at the following link: `http://getbem.com/`.

Now, let us take a look at the CSS required to build this card. I am wrapping the CSS inside another method called `getStyles()` and then I am including it inside the `getTemplate()` method:

```
getStyles() {
  return `
    <style>
      :host {
        display: block;
        font-family: sans-serif;
      }
      :host(.profile-info__emp-type-ft) {
        background-color: #7bb57b;
      }
      :host(.profile-info__emp-type-pt) {
        background-color: #ffc107;
      }
      :host(.profile-info__emp-type-ct) {
        background-color: #03a9f4;
      }

      .profile-info__container {
        display: flex;
        color: white;
        flex-direction: column;
        text-align: center;
      }
      .profile-info__picture {
```

```
      border-radius: 50%;
      width: 80vw;
      height: 80vw;
      margin: 10px auto;
    }
    .profile-info__text {
      padding: 10px;
      flex: 1;
    }
    .profile-info__name {
      font-size: 28px;
    }
    .profile-info__designation {
      font-size: 22px;
      margin-top: 10px;
    }
    .profile-info__id-number {
      margin-top: 10px;
    }
  </style>
  `;
}
```

And let's add the getStyle() method to the getTemplate() method:

```
getTemplate() {
  return `
    ...
    ...
    ...
    ${this.getStyles()}
  `;
}
```

If you look inside the getStyles() method, we have these classes:

- :host(.profile-info__emp-type-ft),
- :host(.profile-info__emp-type-pt), and
- :host(.profile-info__emp-type-ct).

These change the color of the card on the basis of employee type, that is, full-time, part-time, or contractor, respectively.

But we still have no way to add these classes, so we create a new function called `updateCardBackground()` that will be responsible for adding the associated class to the Web Component. And then we will call this class inside the `render()` method:

```
updateCardBackground() {
    this.classList.add(`profile-info__emp-type-${this.getAttribute('employee-
type')}`);
}

render() {
    this.shadowObj.innerHTML = this.getTemplate();

    this.updateCardBackground();
}
```

It is doing nothing but getting the employee type from the attribute and then adding it to the class name of the host.

So if the employee is full-time, then the class becomes `.profile-info__emp-type-ft`; if the employee is part-time, then the class becomes `.profile-info__emp-type-pt`; and if the employee is a contractor, the class becomes `.profile-info__emp-type-ct`. Notice how it is grabbing the employee type from the attribute and appending it to the end of the string `.profile-info__emp-type-`.

Now that we are done with creating the component and styling it, let's add the CSS for larger screens, say tablet and desktop. For the sake of simplicity, we will use the same CSS for desktop and tablet. So, let's add the following CSS to our `getStyles()` method:

```
@media screen and (min-width: 650px) {
    .profile-info__container {
        flex-direction: row;
        text-align: left;
    }
    .profile-info__picture {
        width: 100px;
        height: 100px;
        margin: 10px;
    }
}
```

This makes sure that the Web Component looks like it's from a contact book, the way we see on desktops. And it will show up only when the screen size is more than 650px:

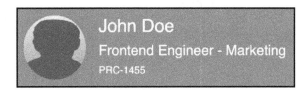

If you are building the Web Component along with this tutorial, try changing the width of the screen.

You can use a similar approach with any of the Web Components and make sure that it looks good when moved from one screen size to another.

Publishing Web Components

If you are developing a Web Component, whether it is for a company, a side project or something that is open source and publicly available, you can make it available for use by other people or team members very easily by publishing your Web Component on the web.

But even before you can publish, you need to make sure that the following steps are completed:

- Your component can be installed via npm
- A proper README file is present in the repository of your component with steps to use and attributes that can be changed
- A demo folder of a working example with index.html file

Let's prepare our file for npm. In order to do that, let's do a quick npm init inside the repo directory with the help of a terminal. I am going to do it with the <profile-info> component that we discussed in the previous section. That will generate a package.json file that looks something like this:

```
{
  "name": "profile-info",
  "version": "0.0.1",
  "description": "A webcomponent that shows information about an employee
in the form of a profile card.",
  "main": "ProfileInfo.js",
  "scripts": {
    "test": "echo \"Error: no test specified\" && exit 1"
```

```
    },
    "keywords": [
      "webcomponent",
      "component",
      "profile",
      "info",
      "employee"
    ],
    "author": "Prateek Jadhwani",
    "license": "ISC",
    "repository": "https://github.com/prateekjadhwani/profile-info"
}
```

We will then create a `ReadMe.md` file in our component directory. And add the following text at the top:

```
[![Published on
webcomponents.org](https://img.shields.io/badge/webcomponents.org-published
-blue.svg)](https://www.webcomponents.org/element/owner/my-element)
```

I added mine with the following:

```
[![Published on
webcomponents.org](https://img.shields.io/badge/webcomponents.org-published-
blue.svg)](https://www.webcomponents.org/element/prateekjadhwani/profile-in
fo)
```

This will create a **published** on **webcomponents.org** site badge that can be viewed by people visiting your GitHub or GitLab page. And it looks something like this:

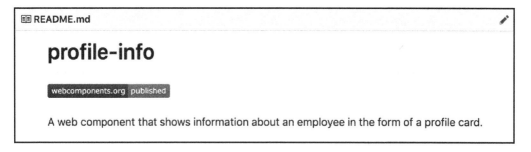

Once this is done, we can set up our `Readme.md` file for a demo section.

You can add to the `Readme.md` file about the attributes, and how it can be used as shown here:

```html
<profile-info
  name="John Doe"
  designation="Frontend Engineer - Marketing"
  id-number="PRC-1455"
  picture-src="./john-doe.png"
  employee-type="ft">
</profile-info>
```

Now you are ready to publish your Web Component on to the NPM JS site. Just type npm `publish` and it will push your code onto the site.

You can find the `<profile-info>` Web Component here at `https://www.npmjs.com/package/profile-info`:

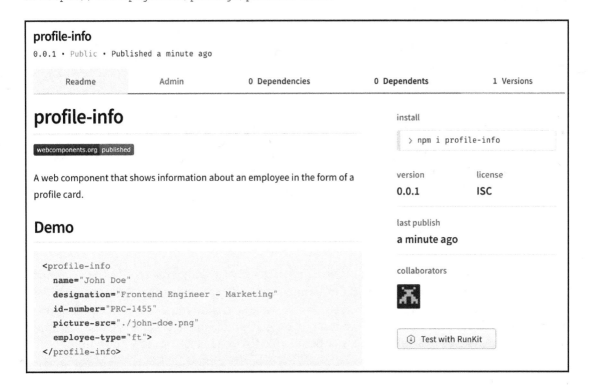

Once you are done with this, you can simply go to `https://www.webcomponents.org/ publish` and scroll down to the section where it says **Ready To Publish?**, and simply put your npm package name and click on the **Publish** button:

This will publish your Web Component, which can be used by anyone. Now your component is available to be distributed across the web.

Extending Web Components – slots

Till now, we have used Web Components with no HTML content inside them. That is, when we import an HTML tag for a Web Component that we created, we have never placed any other HTML tag inside it, for example:

```
<custom header>
    <!-- no html here -->
</custom-header>
```

This creates a huge limitation on the Web Component that we are creating. In the `<custom header>` component, we failed to add dynamic links. You can argue that we can place link data in the form of attributes and then we can run a loop inside our component definition and build the links. But what if we want a button instead of links? What if we want to show user points instead of the button? So, not being able to do these things is a limitation.

In this section, we will extend our current knowledge of Web Components and use the concept of slots to put HTML content inside our Web Components. A slot is a placeholder for any HTML markup that can be placed inside a Web Component. A slot can have a name, and this slot can have HTML or plain text that can be used inside our component.

We will start with the Web Component that we have already worked on, <company-header>. The getTemplate() method of this component is as follows:

```
getTemplate() {
  return `
    <a href="/">
      <img class="icon" src="${this.getAttribute('icon')}" />
    </a>
    <h1 class="heading">${this.getAttribute('page-name')}</h1>
    <div>
      <a class="header-links" href="/home.html">Home</a>
      <a class="header-links" href="/aboutus.html">About Us</a>
    </div>
  `;
}
```

In the preceding code, we can see that there are two links, Home and About Us. If we want to add one more link to this, we will need to modify the definition of the Web Component, which will in turn create problems with maintaining it and we will have to create a new version of it every time we want to add a new link.

In order to solve this problem, we will use slots. We will replace that whole div that contains the links with a slot of name other-links. Let's take a look at the code:

```
getTemplate() {
  return `
    <a href="/">
      <img class="icon" src="${this.getAttribute('icon')}" />
    </a>
    <h1 class="heading">${this.getAttribute('page-name')}</h1>
    <div>
      <slot name="other-links"></slot>
    </div>
  `;
}
```

This way, we can create a slot that can be filled when we use the Web Component:

```
<company-header icon="icon.png" page-name="My Page">
    <ul slot="other-links" class="header-links__container">
      <li>
        <a class="header-links" href="/home.html">Home</a>
      </li>
      <li>
        <a class="header-links" href="/aboutus.html">About Us</a>
      </li>
    </ul>
</company-header>
```

And here, we are filling the slot with a `<ul>` tag that has a `slot` attribute with a value `other-links`. You can have any HTML you want inside this slot. You can even replace it with plain text.

In a Web Component, there can be any number of slots. It totally depends on your use case. But, let us take a look at another example, where we use three slots.

Creating <my-article> Web Component

Let's create a Web Component called `<my-article>` that has three slots: `author`, `article-heading`, and `article`. The definition of the Web Component is as follows starting with the template:

```
getTemplate() {
  return `
    <h1 class="article-heading">
      <slot name="article-heading"></slot>
    </h1>
    <div class="article-author">
      <slot name="author"></slot>
    </div>
    <div class="article-content">
      <slot name="article"></slot>
    </div>
    ${this.getStyle()}
  `;
}
```

As you can see, there are three slots. One for heading, one for author name, and one for content. The `getStyle()` method looks something like this:

```
getStyle() {
  return `
    <style>
      :host {
        display: block;
        background: #e4f4fb;
        padding: 10px;
      }
      .article-heading {
        text-align: right;
        text-transform: lowercase;
        font-size: 50px;
        margin-bottom: 0;
      }
      .article-author {
        text-align: right;
        text-transform: lowercase;
        font-style: italic;
        font-size: 22px;
        padding-bottom: 20px;
        border-bottom: 2px solid black;
      }
      .article-content {
        line-height: 1.5;
        margin-top: 20px;
      }
      .article-content::first-letter {
        font-size: 50px;
        line-height: 0;
      }
    </style>
  `;
}
```

And when we try to use it, it looks something like this:

```
<my-article>
  <span slot="article-heading">A random article</span>
  <span slot="author">Prateek Jadhwani</span>
  <div slot="article">
    <p>This is a demo paragraph</p>
    <p>This is another demo paragraph</p>
  </div>
</my-article>
```

We can of course change the order of the slots while calling the `<my-article>` tag and it will still work as per the definition. The output will look something like this:

a random article

prateek jadhwani

T his is a demo paragraph

This is another demo paragraph

As you can see, we do not have to worry about the look and feel of the content, as long as the classes inside the Web Component are taking care of the styling. This also shows that it is up to the user to use any number of slots.

Summary

In this chapter, we talked about reusability and how we can make sure that our Web Component is as reusable as possible. We even looked at how responsiveness can be incorporated inside a Web Component for maximum reuse.

We learned how to publish our Web Component on the internet as well as a new way of letting dynamic content inside a Web Component with the help of slots.

In the next chapter, we will look into state management, attributes, and how event handling works in a Web Component.

5

Managing States and Props

In the previous chapter, we talked about reusability and how to publish apps on the internet. We also looked into slots and how they can be helpful in extending our Web Components.

In this chapter, we will look into state management. State management lets you keep track of the state a Web Component is in. It is a very useful technique. We will also be looking into attributes to create even better Web Components. We have been using attributes since `Chapter 2`, *Web Components Life Cycle Callback Methods*. But in this chapter, we will look at it from a state management perspective. Then we will be looking into events and event management and how these events can be used to notify users of a Web Component's state.

In this chapter, we will cover the following topics:

- Introduction to State management
- Managing attributes and properties
- Event handling

Introduction to state management

Anything that can be used to manage the state of a **User Interface** (**UI**) can be considered as state management. And we see examples of state management in almost every site that we use on a daily basis. You use Gmail or any other email service. And emails have a state of *read* or *unread*. If you are playing a song on Spotify, the song that you are listening to has a state of *liked* or *not liked*. Based on these states, the UI can be shown in a different manner.

Web Components follow a similar approach. We can use a variable inside our Web Component to keep track of the state. Let's say that we want to create a Web Component that tells the user whether the device that the user is using is online or not. So, the state here will be `isOnline` and its value could be either `online` or `offline`. So let's begin.

Let's call this component <online-checker>, and let's say its state is managed by an internal variable _isOnline. The definition of this component would look something like this:

```
export default class OnlineChecker extends HTMLElement {
  constructor() {

    // We are not even going to touch this.
    super();

    this._isOnline = false;

    // lets create our shadow root
    this.shadowObj = this.attachShadow({mode: 'open'});
  }
}
```

Here, we are setting the initial value of _isOnline to false, because we do not know whether we are online or not.

```
render() {
  this.shadowObj.innerHTML = this.getTemplate();
}

getTemplate() {
  return `
    <span class="online-status online-${this._isOnline ? 'true' :
'false'}"></span>
    <span>${this._isOnline ? 'Online' : 'Offline'}</span>
    ${this.getStyle()}
  `;
}
```

The render() method is the same as our previous examples, nothing special. The special part is the getTemplate() method. Here, we are adding a class online-true or online-false based on the _isOnline variable. We are also adding the text online or offline based on the same.

The getStyle() method looks something like this:

```
getStyle() {
  return `
    <style>
      :host {
        display: inline-block;
        border: 1px solid #cac6c6;
        padding: 10px;
```

```
      border-radius: 5px;
    }
    .online-status {
      height: 10px;
      width: 10px;
      border-radius: 50%;
      display: inline-block;
    }
    .online-true {
      background-color: green;
    }
    .online-false {
      background-color: red;
    }
  </style>
  `;
}
```

The class `.online-true` shows a green circle and `.online-false` shows a red color.

We still have not added the code to check whether the browser is online or not. So let's add it:

```
connectedCallback() {
  this.isOnline = navigator.onLine;
  this.render();
}

set isOnline(value) {
  if(value !== this._isOnline) {
    this._isOnline = value;
    this.render();
  }
}

get isOnline(){
  return this._isOnline;
}
```

Here, we are using `connectedCallback()` to see whether we are online or not. We are using `connectedCallback()` because we want to make sure that this code triggers when the Web Component is on the page.

The `get isOnline()` and `set isOnline()` methods create a property for the component that can be used outside of the component. So, say you have code that looks something like this:

```
document.querySelector('online-checker').isOnline;
```

This will return `true` or `false`, based on the `isOnline` property.

So, we are keeping a track of the online or offline state of the browser inside the `_isOnline` variable and making this value available with the help of the `isOnline` property:

This is a very small introduction to properties inside Web Components as well. We will be looking at more examples in the coming sections.

Attributes and properties

We have been playing around with attributes since the first chapter. And we did get a brief overview of properties and how they can work along with state management to provide a more complete Web Component.

But what is the exact difference between the two? If you are a frontend developer, you must have created a form in your career. We will be looking at an example of an `<input>` tag:

```
<input type="text" value="default value" />
```

If you look at it carefully, we have an attribute called `value` giving it some default value. So if you want to get the value of this `<input>` tag, you can get it by using the following code:

```
document.querySelector('input').getAttribute('value');
```

So, you are directly referencing the attribute for this `<input>` tag to get the value. But there is another way in which you can get this value. And that is as follows:

```
document.querySelector('input').value;
```

This time, we are grabbing the value from the property `value` of the `<input>` tag.

Now the question is, what is the difference? The difference is whether to show it in an attribute or not. There will always be a value that you might not want to show to the HTML code. It may be too long, such as a playlist in a music player Web Component, where the list contains a JSON-style data structure of song names and URLs, or a tax ID number like SSN in a tax registration component, where the data is too sensitive to be put as an attribute.

Let's try to look at this with the help of an example. Let's say we have a Web Component called `<student-list>` where we have an input field that is used to enter student names and a button that lets you add students to the student list. This is what the component looks like:

```
constructor() {

  // We are not even going to touch this.
  super();

  // Initially, the list is empty
  this._list = [];

  // lets create our shadow root
  this.shadowObj = this.attachShadow({mode: 'open'});
  this.render();
}
```

Here, we are managing the student list inside the `_list` variable. The rest is the same as usual:

```
render() {
  this.shadowObj.innerHTML = this.getTemplate();
}

getTemplate() {
  return `
    <div class="student-list__form">
      <input type="text" name="student-name"
        class="student-list__input"
        placeholder="Enter Student Name here"/>
      <button class="js-addButton student-list__add-button">Add
Student</button>
    </div>
    <div class="student-list__student-container">
      <div class="student-list__student-container-heading">Student
List</div>
      <div class="student-list__student-list">
        ${this.getStudents()}
      </div>
```

```
        </div>
        ${this.getStyle()}
      `;
    }
```

As you can see, we have an input field, a button, and a `div student-list__student-list` to put our students in the form of a list:

```
getStudents() {
  return this._list.map((item, num) => {
    return `<div class="student-list__student">${num + 1}. ${item}</div>`;
  }).join('');
}
```

This `getStudents()` method shows the students by running over the `_list` variable that we declared in the `constructor()` method. Let's take a look at our styles before we move on to other sections of this Web Component:

```
getStyle() {
  return `
    <style>
      :host {
        display: block;
      }
      .student-list__form {
        display: flex;
        align-items: center;
      }
      .student-list__input {
        height: 44px;
        margin: 0 25px;
        width: 300px;
        border-radius: 10px;
        border-width: 1px;
        font-size: 18px;
        padding: 0 20px;
      }
      .student-list__add-button {
        height: 50px;
        width: 200px;
        border-radius: 5px;
        display: inline-block;
        border: 1px solid #cac6c6;
      }
      .student-list__student-container {
        margin-top: 50px;
        border-top: 1px solid black;
        padding-top: 50px;
```

```
      font-size: 25px;
    }
    .student-list__student-container-heading {
      margin-bottom: 20px;
    }
    .student-list__student {
      padding: 10px;
      margin-bottom: 10px;
      border-bottom: 1px solid #bfbfbf;
    }
  </style>
  `;
}
```

It's basic CSS, nothing complex. Now, let's add an event listener to our button so that it can add the students to our _list variable:

```
connectedCallback() {

  // what should happen when the button is clicked
  this.shadowObj.querySelector('.js-addButton')
    .addEventListener("click", (e) => {
      this.handleAdd(e);
    });
}

handleAdd() {
  let value = this.shadowObj.querySelector('input[name=student-
name]').value;
  this._list.push(value);
  this.renderList();
}

renderList() {
  this.shadowObj.querySelector('.student-list__student-list').innerHTML
    = this.getStudents();
}
```

Here, we are adding a click event listener to the button .js-addButton. When a user clicks on the button, it grabs the value of the input field, and pushes it to our _list variable. After that, we are simply re-rendering the list; in other words, rather than setting the inner HTML of our component again from scratch, we are simply changing the HTML of the section that needs to be updated.

But what if the user wants to see the student list, or grab it from the component? For this, let's add a property `students` for our user:

```
set students (value) {
  this._list = value;
  this.renderList();
}

get students (){
  return this._list;
}
```

This way, the user can get the student list by using the following code:

```
document.querySelector('student-list').students;
```

This would give the user all the students that have been added in the form of an array:

```
> document.querySelector('student-list').students
  ▶ (3) ["John", "Sam", "Dave"]
```

But now you must be thinking, what if we were to make this available in the attributes? The answer is yes, we can do that. We can update our `handleAdd()` method to something like this:

```
handleAdd() {
  let value = this.shadowObj.querySelector('input[name=student-
name]').value;
  this._list.push(value);
  this.setAttribute("students", this._list);
  this.renderList();
}
```

This will make the list available in an attribute called `students`. But this is what the attribute will look like:

```
▼<student-list students="John,Sam,Dave">
  ▼#shadow-root (open)
    ▼<div class="student-list__form">
        <input type="text" name="student-name" class="student-list__input" placeholder="Enter Student Name here"> == $0
        <button class="js-addButton student-list__add-button">Add Student</button>
      </div>
    ▶<div class="student-list__student-container">…</div>
    ▶<style>…</style>
  </student-list>
```

Do you really want your users to manually parse a string to get an array? What if this data was a little bit more complex? Would the user know what needs to be parsed? In order to solve these complications, we use properties.

I hope this use case will help you decide what to put in properties and what to put in attributes.

Event handling

Till now, we have only looked into button-click events inside our Web Components. This section deals with event handlers from a different perspective.

Let's say we have a Web Component `<custom-clicker>` that has a button and a number that shows the number of times that button has been clicked. Let's take a look at the definition of this Web Component:

```
constructor() {

    // We are not even going to touch this.
    super();

    // Initially, the list is empty
    this._num = 0;

    // lets create our shadow root
    this.shadowObj = this.attachShadow({mode: 'open'});
    this.render();
}
```

We are setting the value of _num to 0. The rest is the same as usual:

```
render() {
    this.shadowObj.innerHTML = this.getTemplate();
}

getTemplate() {
    return `
        <div class="custom-clicker__container">
            <div class="custom-clicker_num">${this.getTimesClicked()}</div>
            <button class="js-button custom-clicker__button">Click Me</button>
        </div>
        ${this.getStyle()}
    `;
}
```

The `render()` and `getTemplate()` methods are pretty much the same as well. We are simply showing text that is obtained via the `getTimesClicked()` method and a button that says **Click Me**:

```
getTimesClicked() {
   return `${this._num} times clicked.`;
}
```

Here, we are simply getting the value of _num and adding informational text. The `getStyle()` method looks something like this:

```
getStyle() {
   return `
     <style>
       :host {
         display: block;
       }
       .custom-clicker__button {
         height: 50px;
         width: 200px;
         border-radius: 5px;
         display: inline-block;
         border: 1px solid #cac6c6;
       }
     </style>
   `;
}
```

We also want to increase the value of _num when the user clicks on the button:

```
connectedCallback() {

   // what should happen when the button is clicked
   this.shadowObj.querySelector('.js-button')
     .addEventListener("click", (e) => {
       this.handleClick(e);
     });
}

handleClick() {
   this._num++;
   this.shadowObj.querySelector('.custom-clicker_num').innerHTML
       = this.getTimesClicked();
}
```

We are simply calling the `handleClick()` method when the user clicks on the button. Then we are simply adding 1 to this _num variable and updating the `.custom-clicker__num` div.

Now, we want to let our user know the value when this button is clicked. We can do so with the help of a custom event. We can do so with the help of `dispatchEvent()`:

```
handleClick() {
  this._num++;
  this.shadowObj.querySelector('.custom-clicker__num').innerHTML
      = this.getTimesClicked();

  this.dispatchEvent(new CustomEvent('change', {
    detail: {
      num: this._num,
    },
    bubbles: true,
  }));
}
```

This notifies the listener to a change in the num variable and can be listened by the following code:

```
<custom-clicker onchange="handleChange(event.detail)"></custom-clicker>

<script type="text/javascript">
  function handleChange(e) {
    console.log(e);
  }
</script>
```

Alternatively, we can use the following code:

```
<custom-clicker></custom-clicker>

<script type="text/javascript">
  document.querySelector('custom-clicker').addEventListener('change', (e)
=> {
    console.log(e.detail);
  });
</script>
```

We can do anything we want with the `e.detail.num` variable.

This way, we can add any number of custom events to notify the user of any changes to the Web Component. The information that needs to be passed on can be put in the `detail` object.

Summary

In this chapter, we looked into various aspects of state management. We went over how attributes and properties can be used to enhance a Web Component. Lastly, we created custom events for our Web Components.

In the next chapter, we will be creating a full fledged single page web app using all the concepts we have learned till now. We will be creating page level Web Components, implement routing and much more.

6
Building a Single Page App using Web Components

So far, we have been using Web Components as an individual entity. But Web Components can be used to make something even more complicated. In this chapter, we will be making a single page web app, solely with the help of Web Components.

In this chapter, we'll cover the following topics:

- Understanding project requirements
- Figuring out reusable Web Components
- Configuring starter project and APIs
- App components
- Other components
- Implementing routing
- Enabling analytics

Understanding project requirements

When it comes to a single-page web app, it can be anything from one page to a thousand pages that you can show on the web app. But for the simplicity of this web app, we will keep it to a maximum of three pages. And the project that we will be trying to create is a GIF collection web app.

We all have been on the internet, and seen how memes and GIFs circulate. In this web app, we will be building something like a GIF repository. The purpose of this web app is to let the user see a list of trending GIFs, search for a specific topic, or maybe see a random GIF.

What we are also going to do is use the GIPHY API to get the GIFs. This way, we won't have to worry about manually scanning the web for GIFs.

Now that we have a basic understanding of our web app and the purpose behind it, let's take a look at how we can convert this requirement into a set of reusable Web Components.

Figuring out reusable Web Components

The main page of the web app we're aiming to create might look something like this:

This page shows that there is a header on top, an input field and a button that can be used to search a string, and a set of results. When we break this page into a set of components, the component list looks something like this:

- **Header component**: A header that can be used on all pages. It needs to be sticky on the top, and clicking on the links should change the URL.
- **GIF cover component**: A component that takes a URL as an attribute and shows it. It can also have a height limit.
- **Search bar component**: A component that is responsible for getting input from a user and searching for a string with the help of APIs. And when the search is complete, it returns the results with the help of a custom event.
- **Search container**: A component that will have a **Search** bar component inside it, and will show GIF cover components based on the result obtained by the **Search** bar.

Let's take a look at the trending page. What this page is supposed to do, just like the search page, is show a collection of GIFs, but instead of making the user search for a specific string, it needs to show the trending GIFs. You should be able to find something similar on the Giphy site: `https://giphy.com/trending-gifs`.

This is what it will look like:

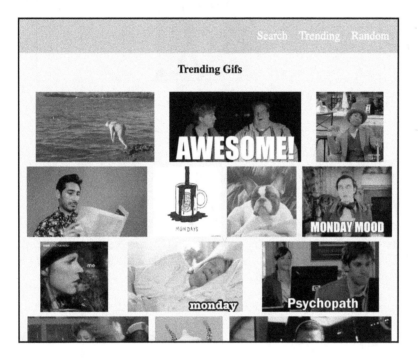

As you can see, it doesn't look that much different from the search page. Let's break down the page into Web Components:

- **Header component**: Same as previously
- **GIF cover**: The same component that we used on the last page to show GIFs
- **Show Trending component**: The container component that will make the call to the API to get trending GIFs and create a collection of GIF Cover components

In all, we will be using just three components for this page.

Let's take a look at the last page. This page is responsible for showing a randomly generated GIF, and this is what it will look like:

As you can see, there is a header at the top, a random GIF, and a button to get another random GIF. Let's break it down into Web Components:

- **Header component**: Same as previously.
- **GIF cover**: Same as the last one, but we won't be seeing a lot of them.
- **Show Random component**: A component that is responsible for making the API call to get a random GIF. It also needs to have a button that needs to trigger the API again when it is clicked.

Now that we know what Web Components are required for this project, let's start working on it.

Configuring the Starter Project and APIs

A starter project is the most minimalistic project that is configured for a single page web app. You can download it from the `Starter Project` directory and put it anywhere on your computer via the following link: `https://github.com/PacktPublishing/Getting-Started-with-Web-Components/tree/master/Chapter06`

Pre-requisites

Before you start using this project, make sure that you have Node.js installed on your computer. You can install it from the Node.js website (`https://nodejs.org/en/`) or, if you want, you can use Homebrew (`https://brew.sh/`) to install it.

Setting up the project

Once you are done installing Node.js, you will need to install certain packages that would make the project work without doing a lot of manual configurations at our end. All the packages are already specified in the `package.json` file. If you want, feel free to look at the contents of this file. The most important package is `webpack`, which is going to be used for bundling our code so that it can be served on a server. Another important package is `node-sass`. It will help us write our code in SCSS.

 I am assuming that you know a little bit of SCSS. It is mostly CSS, but if you get confused, feel free to take a look at the SCSS documentation (`https://sass-lang.com/documentation/syntax`).

You can install the packages involved by typing the following steps in the Terminal:

```
cd Chapter\ 06/Starter\ Project/
npm install
```

This will install all the packages that will be required for this project. It might take a few minutes though, based on the speed of your internet connection.

Running the Starter Project

Now that we have installed all our dependencies, it is time to run the Starter Project and see what it looks like.

To start the project, run the following command in the Terminal:

```
npm start
```

This will show you the following output:

```
> node webpack.dev.server

Hash: ecc08467bc66f8944b6b
Version: webpack 3.12.0
Time: 1284ms
    Asset Size Chunks Chunk Names
bundle.js 19.3 kB 0 [emitted] main
   [0] ./src/index.js 131 bytes {0} [built]
   [1] ./src/styles.scss 1.13 kB {0} [built]
   [2] ./node_modules/css-loader!./node_modules/sass-
loader/lib/loader.js!./src/styles.scss 225 bytes {0} [built]
   [3] ./node_modules/css-loader/lib/css-base.js 2.26 kB {0} [built]
```

```
    [4] ./node_modules/style-loader/lib/addStyles.js 8.7 kB {0} [built]
    [5] ./node_modules/style-loader/lib/urls.js 3.01 kB {0} [built]
    [6] ./src/components/my-app/index.js 541 bytes {0} [built]
webpack: Compiled successfully.
```

This means that webpack is done creating a `bundle.js` file from the six listed files. And, you can simply go to a browser and open the following URL: `http://localhost:3000`.

This will show our starter project with the text **My App**.

Pre-requisite for API calls

You, as a user, will need to register for an API key and this can be done by following the steps as shown here:

1. Go to the following URL and register for a free account: `https://developers.giphy.com`
2. Once you are done creating an account, create an app by clicking on the **Create New App** button at the top, as follows:

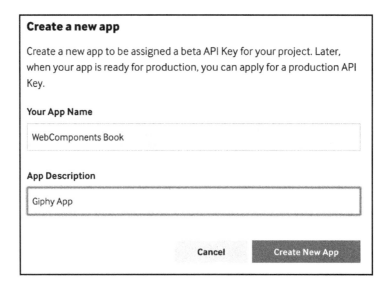

3. Once you are done creating the app, you will be dropped onto a dashboard page where you can see your registered apps along with the API key required, as shown in the following screenshot:

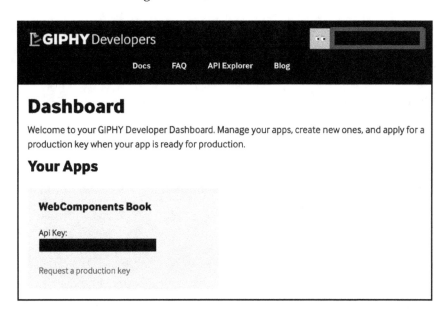

If you have a moment, feel free to take a look at the API docs: `https://developers.giphy.com/docs/`.

But you don't have to worry about the APIs too much; we will be talking about this when we talk about components.

App components

Before we take a look at the `<my-app>` component, let's take a look at what happens when you go to `localhost:3000`. The `index.html` file runs. The contents of `index.html` look something like this:

```
<html>
  <head>
    <title>My App</title>
  </head>
  <body>
```

```
        <my-app></my-app>
        <script src="bundle.js"></script>
    </body>
</html>
```

As you can see, it is trying to render the `<my-app>` component. But it tries to get the definition of `MyApp` from the `bundle.js` file. This `bundle.js` file, as discussed earlier, is a collection of all the components that are required on the page and will be required by the `<my-app>` component. This `bundle.js` file is created with the help of webpack. And the configuration of the `bundle.js` file can be found in the `webpack.config.js` file, which looks something like this:

```
entry: './src/index.js',
```

The entry file that is chosen is the `/src/index.js` file. But then again, where does the `bundle.js` part come from? If you look at the bottom in the `webpack.config.js` file, you will see something like this:

```
output: {
  filename: 'bundle.js',
  path: path.resolve(__dirname, 'dist')
},
```

Here, we are making sure that everything that is inside the entry file, `/src/index.js`, gets written to the `bundle.js` file. You can definitely modify this file if you have experience with webpack. But for the sake of simplicity, we are going to leave it as is.

Let's take a look at the `/src/index.js` file:

```
import './styles.scss';

import MyApp from './components/my-app';
customElements.define('my-app', MyApp);
```

What we are seeing here is that, it is importing a `styles.scss` file, which can be used to store our global styles, and then it is importing our `MyApp` class from the `/components/my-app` folder. And then, it defines the custom element. This is something that we have already looked into in Chapter 1, *Web Components Essentials and Specifications*.

If we look into the `MyApp` class, we will find that there is nothing different than what we have already learned in the previous chapters.

The `constructor()` method is no different:

```
constructor() {

    // We are not even going to touch this.
    super();

    // lets create our shadow root
    this.shadowObj = this.attachShadow({mode: 'open'});
    this.render();
}
```

The `render()` method is pretty simple as well:

```
render() {
    this.shadowObj.innerHTML = this.getTemplate();
}
```

The `getStyle()` and `getTemplate()` methods are the same as well; no different from what we have learned previously:

```
getTemplate() {
    return `
      <div>
        My App
      </div>
      ${this.getStyle()}
    `;
}

getStyle() {
    return `
      <style>
        :host {
          display: block;
        }
      </style>
    `;
}
```

With the help of the code here, we can understand how the app component works and how it is the most important Web Component in order to make our single page web app work.

Functional components

Now that we know what the <my-app> component looks like and what it needs to work, let's start writing the components that we discussed in the beginning of this chapter.

The <gif-cover> Web Component

As discussed earlier, the purpose of this web component is to show a GIF. And, from the screenshots, we can see that it is one of the most reusable components of the project. So, let's start writing its code:

```
export default class GifCover extends HTMLElement {
  constructor() {

    // We are not even going to touch this.
    super();

    // lets get the url from attribute
    this.url = this.getAttribute('url');

    // lets create our shadow root
    this.shadowObj = this.attachShadow({mode: 'open'});

    this.render();
  }

  ...
}
```

In the constructor(), we are using this.url to grab the URL from the attribute. We will be using this URL as a source for the image, as shown in the following code:

```
render() {
  this.shadowObj.innerHTML = this.getTemplate();
}

getTemplate() {
  return `
    <div>
      <img class="gif-cover__image"
        src="${this.url}" />
    </div>
    ${this.getStyle()}
  `;
}
```

We will also need styles for this component; we can achieve this by adding the following:

```
getStyle() {
  return `
    <style>
      :host {
        display: block;
      }
      .gif-cover__image {
        height: 150px;
      }
    </style>
  `;
}
```

As you can see, the only limitation that we are putting on this component is the image height. You can definitely remove it if you don't like it.

Once our `<gif-cover>` web component is done, we can move on to another web component.

The <search-bar> Web Component

If we take a look at the **Search** page, we will see that there is a search bar. The input field and the **Search** button are a part of this `<search-bar>` component and are responsible for making API calls.

The API call that we will be using here is the GIPHY Search Endpoint API, `https://api.giphy.com/v1/gifs/search`.

 The preceding link is an API link. You cannot access it directly, but you can use it to grab data if you have a key.

You will need to provide it with your key, which can be obtained from your dashboard. And, you may want to take a look at the docs here: `https://developers.giphy.com/docs/#operation--gifs-search-get`.

When you make a call to this API, it is going to return an array of objects, each representing a GIF and its metadata.

Now that we know what API to use, let's take a look at the code:

```
export default class SearchBar extends HTMLElement {

  constructor() {

    // We are not even going to touch this.
    super();

    this.key = 'YOUR-KEY';
    this.searchUrl = 'https://api.giphy.com/v1/gifs/search';
    this.showlimit = 20;

    // lets create our shadow root
    this.shadowObj = this.attachShadow({mode: 'open'});

    this.render();
  }

  ...
  ...

}
```

The `constructor()` method contains your key (which you will get from the GIPHY dashboard), the search URL, which is the API URL, and the limit or the amount to show in one call. Let's take a look at the `render()` method:

```
render() {
  this.shadowObj.innerHTML = this.getTemplate();
}

getTemplate() {
  return `
    <div class="search-bar__container">
      <input type="text"
        class="search-bar__search-field"
        placeholder="Enter Search Text Here">
      <button class="search-bar__button">Search</button>
    </div>
    ${this.getStyle()}
  `;
}
```

It is nothing unusual. We just have a text field and a button. And the styles look something like this:

```
getStyle() {
  return `
    <style>
      :host {
        display: block;
      }
      .search-bar__container {
        display: flex;
      }
      .search-bar__search-field {
        flex: 1;
        margin: 10px;
        height: 50px;
        font-size: 18px;
        padding: 10px;
        border-radius: 5px;
        border: none;
        color: #8e8e8e;
      }
      .search-bar__button {
        margin: 10px;
        width: 200px;
        border: none;
        font-size: 18px;
        color: #5f5f5f;
        cursor: pointer;
      }
      .search-bar__button:hover {
        background: #68f583;
      }
    </style>
  `;
}
```

Along with basic rendering, we will also need to add a click event for the button, so that it can make a call to the API:

```
connectedCallback() {
  this.shadowObj.querySelector('button')
    .addEventListener('click', (e) => {
      this.handleSearch();
    });
}
```

This way, when a user clicks on the button, it is going to trigger the `handleSearch()` method, which looks something like this:

```
handleSearch() {
  let value = this.shadowObj.querySelector('input').value;

  fetch(`${this.searchUrl}?api_key=${this.key}&q=${value}&limit=${this.showli
  mit}`)
    .then(response => response.json())
    .then((jsonResponse) => {
      this.dispatchDataInEvent(jsonResponse.data);
    });


}
```

Here, in the `handleSearch()` function, we are first getting the value of the input field. This is the value that the user entered. Then, we are making a call to the API by concatenating the API URL. The URL looks like the following:

```
`${this.searchUrl}?api_key=${this.key}&q=${value}&limit=${this.showlimit}`
```

This will get the URL from the `searchUrl` variable, and the key from the `key` variable. The `value` is obtained from the input field. And the limit is obtained from the `showlimit` variable.

Once the call is made, and the promise resolves, it will call the `dispatchDataInEvent()` method:

```
dispatchDataInEvent(data) {
  this.dispatchEvent(new CustomEvent('search-complete', {
    detail: {
      data: data,
    },
    bubbles: true,
  }));
}
```

This `dispatchDataInEvent()` method will be responsible for notifying the parent Web Component of the new data that is obtained after the call.

Now that we have created Web Components that can be reused in the `<search-container>` component, let's take a look at `<search-container>`.

The <search-container> Web Component

Since the <search-container> component is going to use the <gif-cover> and
<search-bar> components, the outline of our component will look something like this:

```
import SearchBar from '../search-bar';
import GifCover from '../gif-cover';

export default class SearchContainer extends HTMLElement {
    ...
    ...
    ...
}
```

We are simply importing the classes of the Web Components that are going to be used in
this component. This is pretty much the exact same thing that we have used in our
index.html files.

Let's take a look at the constructor() method:

```
constructor() {

    // We are not even going to touch this.
    super();

    // lets create our shadow root
    this.shadowObj = this.attachShadow({mode: 'open'});

    this.registerOtherComponents();
    this.render();
}
```

Here, we have a registerOtherComponents() method that we are calling before the
render() method. This is also the first time we are registering a custom element inside
another custom element:

```
registerOtherComponents() {
    if (typeof customElements.get('search-bar') === 'undefined') {
        customElements.define('search-bar', SearchBar);
    }

    if (typeof customElements.get('gif-cover') === 'undefined') {
        customElements.define('gif-cover', GifCover);
    }
}
```

Here, we are first checking if the component has already been registered or not. If it has not been registered yet, then it registers it. Usually, a browser spits out an error message if it tries to register a custom element twice. This check is to fix that problem.

Once we are done registering the Web Components, it's time to render:

```
render() {
    this.shadowObj.innerHTML = this.getTemplate();
}

getTemplate() {
    return `
        <div class="search-container__container">
            <search-bar></search-bar>
            <div class="search-container__images">
                <p>Try Searching for a tag in the search bar</p>
            </div>
        </div>
        ${this.getStyle()}
    `;
}
```

Here, we are rendering the `<search-bar>` component, but we do not see the `<gif-cover>` component. This is because the `<gif-cover>` components are to be shown only when data is retrieved from the `<search-bar>` component, and that is done when the `<search-bar>` component dispatches a `search-complete` event. Let's take a look at the `connectedCallback()` callback to add this event handler:

```
connectedCallback() {
    this.shadowObj.querySelector('search-bar')
        .addEventListener('search-complete', (e) => {
            this.handleSearchData(e.detail.data);
        });
}
```

Here, we are looking for the `<search-bar>` element and adding an event listener. When that event occurs, it is going to trigger the `handleSearchData()` method and pass the associated data into it:

```
handleSearchData(data) {
    data = data.map((val, index) => {
        return `
          <gif-cover url=${val.images.downsized_medium.url}></gif-cover>
        `;
    }).join('');
    this.shadowObj.querySelector('.search-container__images')
        .innerHTML = data;
}
```

Just like the student list example in the previous chapters, here we are creating an HTML collection of `<gif-cover>` Web Components with the URL obtained from the `data` array, and then appending this HTML to the `search-container__images` div. This will also make sure to replace the `<gif-cover>` with new data when the user searches for something else.

Also, the `getStyles()` method is important. This is what it looks like:

```
getStyle() {
    return `
      <style>
        :host {
          display: block;
        }
        .search-container__container {
          display: block;
          padding: 10px;
        }
        .search-container__images {
          display: flex;
          padding: 10px;
          flex-wrap: wrap;
          box-sizing: border-box;
          justify-content: space-evenly;
        }
        gif-cover {
          flex-basis: 10%;
          padding: 5px;
        }
      </style>
    `;
}
```

Now that we have our `<search-container>` Web Component all set, let's add it to the `<my-app>` component, as shown here:

```
getTemplate() {
  return `
    <search-container></search-container>
    ${this.getStyle()}
  `;
}
```

Also, don't forget to register the component, as shown in the following:

```
if (typeof customElements.get('search-container') === 'undefined') {
  customElements.define('search-container', SearchContainer);
}
```

This way, we can make sure that `SearchContainer` is initialized only once.

Feel free to run the code and see if you are able to see a search bar; clicking on the search button will return some results.

Let's take a look at the `<show-trending>` component.

The `<show-trending>` Web Component

The purpose of the `<show-trending>` Web Component is to first make a call to the API and then show the most trending GIFs. For this component, the API that we will be using is, `https://api.giphy.com/v1/gifs/trending`.

Like the previous API, this also returns an array of objects that contains the URL and other metadata. To take a look at the documentation for this API, visit this link: `https://developers.giphy.com/docs/#operation--gifs-trending-get`.

Now that we know how the API works, lets take a look at the code for the `<show-trending>` Web Component:

```
export default class ShowTrending extends HTMLElement {

  constructor() {

    // We are not even going to touch this.
    super();

    this.key = 'YOUR_KEY';
    this.url = 'https://api.giphy.com/v1/gifs/trending';
```

```
    this.showlimit = 20;

    // lets create our shadow root
    this.shadowObj = this.attachShadow({mode: 'open'});

    this.registerOtherComponents();
    this.render();

  }

  ...
  ...

}
```

Here, just like the `<search-bar>` components, we have a `key` variable for YOUR_KEY, the URL to store the API call, and the `showlimit` variable to set the max amount of data that can come from the API call.

We have already seen how our `registerOtherComponents()` method should work, as follows:

```
registerOtherComponents() {
  if (typeof customElements.get('gif-cover') === 'undefined') {
    customElements.define('gif-cover', GifCover);
  }
}
```

Also, don't forget to import the `GifCover` component:

```
import GifCover from '../gif-cover';
```

Let's take a look at the `render()` method:

```
render() {
  this.shadowObj.innerHTML = this.getTemplate();
}

getTemplate() {
  return `
    <div class="show-trending__container">
      <h2 class="show-trending__heading">Trending Gifs</h2>
      <div class="show-trending__images"></div>
    </div>
    ${this.getStyle()}
  `;
}
```

Here, we just have a `show-trending__images` div that will have `<gif-cover>` Web Components once the API call is made.

The `getStyles()` method looks something like this:

```
getStyle() {
  return `
    <style>
      :host {
        display: block;
      }
      .show-trending__heading {
        text-align: center;
      }
      .show-trending__images {
        display: flex;
        padding: 10px;
        flex-wrap: wrap;
        box-sizing: border-box;
        justify-content: space-evenly;
      }

      gif-cover {
        flex-basis: 10%;
        padding: 5px;
      }
    </style>
  `;
}
```

Now that we have the component set up, it is time to make sure that the component makes the API call:

```
connectedCallback() {
  this.makeApiCall();
}

makeApiCall() {
  fetch(`${this.url}?api_key=${this.key}&limit=${this.showlimit}`)
    .then(response => response.json())
    .then((jsonResponse) => {
      this.handleTrendingData(jsonResponse.data);
    });

}
```

What we are doing is simply making the call when the component is connected and DOM is added to the page. Once we have the data from the `fetch` call, we pass this data to the `handleTrendingData()` method:

```
handleTrendingData(data) {

    data = data.map((val, index) => {
        return `
          <gif-cover url=${val.images.downsized_medium.url}></gif-cover>
        `;
    }).join('');

    this.shadowObj.querySelector('.show-trending__images')
        .innerHTML = data;
}
```

As you can see, this `handleTrendingData()` method is responsible for creating `<gif-cover>` Web Components, giving them GIF URLs, and adding them to the `show-trending__images` div.

Just like the `<search-container>` component, you can test the `<show-trending>` component inside the `<my-app>` component.

The `<show-random>` Web Component

Just like the `<show-trending>` Web Component, this is a container Web Component. That means it will be using other components in a nested way. The component that it will be using is `<gif-cover>`. Let's see what the outline looks like:

```
import GifCover from '../gif-cover';

export default class ShowRandom extends HTMLElement {
    . . .
    . . .
    . . .
}
```

And, the `constructor()` method looks something like this:

```
constructor() {

    // We are not even going to touch this.
    super();

    // the key required for api
```

```
    this.key = 'YOUR_KEY';

    // the url used to get the random gif
    this.url = 'https://api.giphy.com/v1/gifs/random';

    // lets create our shadow root
    this.shadowObj = this.attachShadow({mode: 'open'});

    this.registerOtherComponents();
    this.render();
}
```

Here, the API that we are using is, `https://api.giphy.com/v1/gifs/random`.

Unlike the previous APIs, this one spits out only one object at a time. This object will have the URL and other metadata associated with a GIF. If you need more information on it, feel free to refer to the documentation: `https://developers.giphy.com/docs/#operation--gifs-random-get`

The `registerOtherComponents()` method looks exactly the same as the previous one:

```
registerOtherComponents() {
  // lets register other components used
  if (typeof customElements.get('gif-cover') === 'undefined') {
    customElements.define('gif-cover', GifCover);
  }
}
```

Also, the `render()` method looks something like this:

```
render() {
  this.shadowObj.innerHTML = this.getTemplate();
}

getTemplate() {
  return `
    <div class="show-random__container">
      <div class="show-random__images"></div>
      <button class="show-random__button">Get Another Random
      Image</button>
    </div>
    ${this.getStyle()}
  `;
}
```

Here, we see that we have a div, `show-random__images`, to show the random image. And, there is a button right below it. The `getStyle()` method looks like this:

```
getStyle() {
  return `
    <style>
      :host {
        display: block;
      }
      .show-random__container {
        text-align: center;
      }
      .show-random__images {
        display: flex;
        padding: 10px;
        flex-wrap: wrap;
        box-sizing: border-box;
        justify-content: space-evenly;
      }

      .show-random__button {
        margin: 10px;
        border: none;
        font-size: 18px;
        color: #5f5f5f;
        cursor: pointer;
        padding: 10px;
      }

      gif-cover {
        flex-basis: 10%;
        padding: 5px;
      }
    </style>
  `;
}
```

Now that the component is set up, let's make the API call:

```
connectedCallback() {
  this.handleRandom();
}

handleRandom() {
  fetch(`${this.url}?api_key=${this.key}`)
  .then(response => response.json())
  .then((jsonResponse) => {
    this.handleTrendingData(jsonResponse.data);
  });

}
```

This `handleRandom()` function is responsible for making the API call, and when the data is retrieved, it passes it to the `handleTrendingData()` method:

```
handleTrendingData(data) {

  this.shadowObj.querySelector('.show-random__images')
    .innerHTML = `
      <gif-cover url=${data.image_url}></gif-cover>
    `;
}
```

We also need to make sure that the image refreshes when the button is clicked. So, we can add this event listener inside the `connectedCallback()` method to make it work:

```
connectedCallback() {
  this.handleRandom();

  this.shadowObj.querySelector('button')
    .addEventListener('click', (e) => {
      this.handleRandom();
    });
}
```

This way, whenever the button is clicked, it will trigger the `handleRandom()` method again.

The <my-app> component

Just like the <show-trending> and <search-container> components, you can test the <show-random> Web Component by adding the <show-random> component inside the <my-app> component. But if you want to integrate it all, I have a better option.

Let's take a look at the <my-app> component. If we want all these three components, we will need to include it first:

```
import SearchContainer from '../search-container';
import ShowTrending from '../show-trending';
import ShowRandom from '../show-random';

export default class MyApp extends HTMLElement {
    ...
    ...
    ...
}
```

Now that we have these components imported, lets register these custom elements:

```
registerOtherComponents() {
  if (typeof customElements.get('search-container') === 'undefined') {
    customElements.define('search-container', SearchContainer);
  }

  if (typeof customElements.get('show-trending') === 'undefined') {
    customElements.define('show-trending', ShowTrending);
  }

  if (typeof customElements.get('show-random') === 'undefined') {
    customElements.define('show-random', ShowRandom);
  }
}
```

We can also add a showSection variable to keep track of what component to show at what time:

```
constructor() {
  ...

  // to show what section
  this.shownSection = 1;

  ...
}
```

We are initially setting it to a value of 1, so that it can show `<search-container>` by default.

And, to make it work, we will modify the `getTemplate()` method a little bit to look something like this:

```
getTemplate() {
  return `
    <div class="app-section">
      ${this.getSection(this.shownSection)}
    </div>
    ${this.getStyle()}
  `;
}

getSection(section) {
  switch(section) {
    case 1:
      return `
        <search-container></search-container>
      `;
    case 2:
      return `
        <show-trending></show-trending>
      `;
    case 3:
      return `
        <show-random></show-random>
      `;
  }
}
```

This way, you can test the pages manually by changing the value of `showSection`.

Now that we have created a way where we can show different page level components by changing the value of the variable `showSections`, we can now concentrate on the routing aspect of these page level components. Rather than manually changing the page numbers, it is time to automate this page change concept with the implementation of routing.

Implementing routing

Until now, we have been manually changing the code to see different pages of our single-page web app. Also, we have not talked about the header component yet. In this section, we will take a look at the header component, update the URLs based on the link, and make sure our page view changes based on the link clicked.

So, let's take a look at the `<custom-header>` component:

```
constructor() {

  // We are not even going to touch this.
  super();

  // lets create our shadow root
  this.shadowObj = this.attachShadow({mode: 'open'});

  this.render();
}
```

The `constructor()` method is straightforward. Let's take a look at the `render()` method:

```
render() {
  this.shadowObj.innerHTML = this.getTemplate();
}

getTemplate() {
  return `
    <ul class="custom-header__ul">
      <li class="custom-header__li">
        <a href="#search">Search</a>
      </li>
      <li class="custom-header__li">
        <a href="#trending">Trending</a>
      </li>
      <li class="custom-header__li">
        <a href="#random">Random</a>
      </li>
    </ul>
    ${this.getStyle()}
  `;
}
```

As you can see, we have three links: **Search**, **Trending**, and **Random**. Clicking on these links also changes the URL hash:

```
getStyle() {
  return `
    <style>
      :host {
        display: block;
        top: 0;
        background: #46cff3;
        position: sticky;
        height: 75px;
      }
      .custom-header__ul {
        display: flex;
        margin: 0;
        justify-content: flex-end;
        height: 100%;

      }
      .custom-header__li {
        align-self: center;
        list-style-type: none;
        margin-right: 25px;
      }

      .custom-header__li a {
        text-decoration: none;
        color: white;
        font-size: 25px;
      }
    </style>
  `;
}
```

The styles are pretty simple as well.

Let's take a look at the event handlers for the click. For routing, we will need to notify the <my-app> Web Component (where this <custom-header> component is going to be used) about the click event or what link the user clicked on:

```
connectedCallback() {
  this.shadowObj.querySelectorAll('.custom-header__li a')
    .forEach((aTag, index) => {
      aTag.addEventListener('click', (e) => {
        this.handleClick(index);
      });
    });
}
```

Here, we are simply binding a click event to all the links and making sure that the handleClick() method is triggered, along with the index of the link:

```
handleClick(index) {
  this.dispatchEvent(new CustomEvent('custom-header-clicked', {
    detail: {
      data: index + 1,
    },
    bubbles: true,
  }));
}
```

This handleClick() method simply passes this index value to the parent component trying to listen to the custom-header-clicked event.

Inside the <my-app> component, the definition will update as well. For example, we will need to import the CustomHeader class:

```
import CustomHeader from '../custom-header';
```

We will also need to update the registerOtherComponents() method by adding the following line:

```
if (typeof customElements.get('custom-header') === 'undefined') {
  customElements.define('custom-header', CustomHeader);
}
```

This will also update the `getTemplate()` method, and make it look like this:

```
getTemplate() {
  return `
    <custom-header></custom-header>
    <div class="app-section">
      ${this.getSection(this.shownSection)}
    </div>
    ${this.getStyle()}
  `;
}
```

Here, we are simply adding the `<custom-header>` element. We will also need to capture the event emitter by this element:

```
connectedCallback() {
  this.shadowObj.querySelector('custom-header')
    .addEventListener('custom-header-clicked', (e) => {
      let newShownSection = e.detail.data;
      if(newShownSection !== this.shownSection) {
        this.shownSection = newShownSection;
        this.reRenderAppSection();
      }
    })
}
```

We are adding an event listener to the `custom-header` element and making sure that the last value of `showSection` is not equal to the newer one. If it is not, then update the value and call the `reRenderAppSection()` method:

```
reRenderAppSection() {
  this.shadowObj.querySelector('.app-section').innerHTML =
    this.getSection(this.shownSection);
}
```

This `reRenderAppSection()` method simply update the view based on the `showSection` variable.

Now, you can go ahead and test it on the browser by clicking on the header links, and watch the pages change. You can also see the URL changing in the address bar. Even though this all sounds complete, I would like to add one more feature to the routing.

Note the URL that you see in the address bar. If you send the URL with trending in the hash to someone, would it open the trending page? The answer is no. The same applies for the URL with random in the hash. It won't work. We need to have an extra piece of code:

```
handleURL() {
  switch(window.location.hash) {
    case '#search':
      this.shownSection = 1;
      break;
    case '#trending':
      this.shownSection = 2;
      break;
    case '#random':
      this.shownSection = 3;
      break;
    default:
      this.shownSection = 1;
      break;
  }

  this.render();
}
```

You can call this `handleURL()` method in the `constructor()` method, and see it working. It updates the value of the `showSection` variable and, this way, the `getSection()` method in `getTemplate()` knows what page to render.

Now that the app is built, let's try adding some extra features that will make our single page web app more useful.

Enabling analytics

Analytics play an important role in understanding what users are visiting your site and how long they have been on a particular page. In this section, we will be using Google Analytics to track user interactions on the site. This is one of those really easy things that you can do even outside of Web Components.

In order to start using Analytics, we need to do the following:

1. Go to `https://analytics.google.com/,` then click on the **admin** button and create a new property. You will be dropped on to New Property page.

2. You can then start filling out the forms on the page:

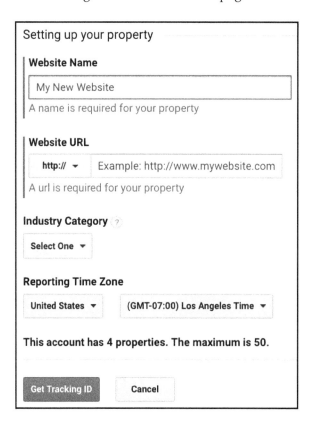

3. Once you have filled in the details, and clicked on the **Get Tracking ID** button, you will be dropped onto the next page:

Tracking ID

UA-65947202-5

Status

No data received in past 48 hours. Learn more

Website Tracking

Global Site Tag (gtag.js)

This is the Global Site Tag (gtag.js) tracking code for this property. Copy and paste this code as the first item into the <HEAD> of every webpage you want to track. If you already have a Global Site Tag on your page, simply add the *config* line from the snippet below to your existing Global Site Tag.

```
<!-- Global site tag (gtag.js) - Google Analytics -->
<script async src="https://www.googletagmanager.com/gtag/js?id=UA-65947202-5"></script>
<script>
  window.dataLayer = window.dataLayer || [];
  function gtag(){dataLayer.push(arguments);}
  gtag('js', new Date());

  gtag('config', 'UA-65947202-5');
</script>
```

The Global Site Tag provides streamlined tagging across Google's site measurement, conversion tracking, and remarketing products – giving you better control while making implementation easier. By using gtag.js, you will be able to benefit from the latest dynamic features and integrations as they become available. Learn more

---

4. You can use the code from the text area and put it in your `index.html` file.
5. That's it. Now, you can simply go to the following URL and see how users are visiting your site: `https://analytics.google.com`.

6. You will be dropped onto a page where you can see how users have visited your page:

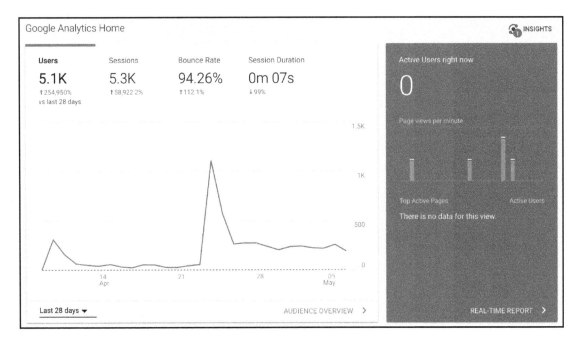

And, you can then use this data to understand what users do on your page, and how much time they stay on the site.

Summary

In this chapter, we created a single page web app using just Web Components. We learned how to break down a page into atomic and container Web Components. We learned how to include atomic components in a strategic way, so that they can be reused in an efficient way. We even looked into routing and how it can be used to keep track of what page the user is on. Lastly, we discussed how to integrate analytics into our single page web app, and how it can be used to understand different types of users. You should now be able to create any single page web application based on the concepts above without any problems.

In the next chapter, we will look into Polymer and Stencil JS, which are libraries that use Web Components, and how the code differs from what we have learned so far.

7
Implementing Web Components using Polymer and Stencil

Up until now, we have built components using vanilla JavaScript with no dependencies. But sometimes, companies make a decision to use libraries that can help ease the workflow. In this chapter, we will look into two different libraries: Polymer and Stencil. In the background, these two libraries use Web Components, but both of them come with their own features. Let's dive into these libraries.

In this chapter, we're going to cover the following topics:

- Polymer
- Stencil

Polymer

Polymer is a library that lets you create custom elements in a really easy way. It comes with a set of features that can be used to create shadow DOM, add events, and use attributes and properties just like we have learned in previous chapters.

You can find the Polymer project at the following URL: `https://Polymer-library.Polymer-project.org/`.

A major difference between the vanilla Web Components and Polymer is that Polymer comes with its own data system. That means you can make various computations and manipulations to the component based on this data. You can observe attribute and property changes, and you can even do two-way data binding, something that is missing from vanilla Web Components. The presence of these features helps with a lot of use cases, and helps with making the life of a developer easier.

We will now take a look at how to use Polymer in more detail.

Hello World in Polymer

Unlike vanilla Web Components, Polymer is a library that needs to be installed. But before we even have the library installed, we will be needing Polymer's **Command Line Interface (CLI)** that come with its own server and testing framework. We can install it using the following command:

```
npm install -g Polymer-cli
```

And, once installed, you can check if it is installed by using the following command:

```
Polymer --version
```

Now that Polymer is installed, let's try to create a `<hello-world>` component using this library. Let's create a folder called `HelloWorld` and then create a file called `index.html`. The contents of this file can be very basic, like the following:

```
<!DOCTYPE html>
<html lang="en" dir="ltr">
 <head>
    <meta charset="utf-8">
    <title>Hello World</title>
  </head>
  <body>
    <p>You stuff goes here.</p>
  </body>
</html>
```

In order to run this file, instead of using `SimpleHTTPServer`, we will use a server that is provided by `Polymer-cli` itself. We can run the server by using the following command:

```
Polymer serve
```

Once you run this command, you should get a console output this in the Terminal:

```
info: Files in this directory are available under the following URLs
  applications: http://127.0.0.1:8081
  reusable components: http://127.0.0.1:8081/components/Polymer/
```

This shows that the server is running, and you can see the index.html file running on http://127.0.0.1:8081/.

Now that our server is running and Polymer is installed, let's start writing our <hello-world> Polymer component.

Since we are going to use the Polymer library, let's install the library for this project:

```
npm i @Polymer/Polymer
```

Also, let's create a file called hello-world.js. The contents of this file are as follows:

```
import { PolymerElement, html } from '@Polymer/Polymer/Polymer-element.js';

class HelloWorld extends PolymerElement {
    ...
    ...
    ...
}

customElements.define('hello-world', HelloWorld);
```

Here, we are simply importing Polymer library that we just installed using npm command. Also, instead of using HTMLElement, we are using PolymerElement. And then, we are registering the class as a custom element.

The class definition will be a little bit different than vanilla Web Components:

```
class HelloWorld extends PolymerElement {
  constructor() {
    super();
  }

  static get template() {
    return html`
      <p>Hello World</p>
    `;
  }
}
```

Here, we have the `constructor()` method, just like vanilla Web Components, but the `super()` method call doesn't have `props` in it. Also, we are not manually calling the `render()` method. Instead, the code is rendered automatically from the `template()` property.

We also need to keep in mind that unlike vanilla Web Components, we are not manually creating the shadow DOM for a Polymer element. Here, we use the `html` object from the `Polymer` library to stamp the `html` to the element's shadow DOM.

Now that the component is created, we can use it in our `index.html` file in the following way:

```html
<!DOCTYPE html>
<html lang="en" dir="ltr">
  <head>
    <meta charset="utf-8">
    <title>Hello World</title>
    <script type="module" src="hello-world.js"></script>
  </head>
  <body>
    <hello-world></hello-world>
  </body>
</html>
```

Here, we are simply importing the `hello-world.js` file, and then using the `<hello-world>` element directly.

As you can see, the `Polymer` library helps a lot when it comes to saving the lines of code. And, with this example, you now know how to create a Polymer element. You can also try creating other elements that we have studied in the previous chapters.

Nested elements in Polymer

In the previous chapters, we looked at how different Web Components are used inside other Web Components to create complex and nested components. This methodology is not just limited to vanilla Web Components. We can use it inside Polymer components as well.

Let's say we have another `PolymerElement` that looks like this:

```js
// second-element.js

import { PolymerElement, html } from '@Polymer/Polymer/Polymer-element.js';

class SecondElement extends PolymerElement {
```

```
constructor() {
  super();
}
static get template() {
  return html`
    <style>
      p {
        color: red;
      }
    </style>
    <p>This is the second element</p>
  `;
  }
}
```

```
customElements.define('second-element', SecondElement);
```

As you can see, it is not a complex element. In fact, it looks a lot like the `<hello-world>` element. Now, let's say we want to include this `<second-element>` in the `<hello-world>` element. We can do it by changing the `<hello-world>` code in the following way:

```
import { PolymerElement, html } from '@Polymer/Polymer/Polymer-element.js';
import './second-element.js';

class HelloWorld extends PolymerElement {
  constructor() {
    super();
  }
  static get template() {
    return html`
      <p>Hello World</p>
      <second-element></second-element>
    `;
  }
}
```

```
customElements.define('hello-world', HelloWorld);
```

Here, you can see that we are importing the code from the `./second-element.js` file. And we are simply using it with the help of the `<second-element>` HTML code. It is that simple.

Also, if you notice the definition of the `<second-element>` class, you can see that we have used a style tag as well. We can make use of all the styles that we have studied in the previous chapters.

Attributes and properties in Polymer

In the previous chapters, we saw how attributes and properties help make our Web Components better. They help with passing data, as well as keep track of the element's state. Similarly, we can do the same for elements built using Polymer as well.

Let's take a look at how properties work in Polymer. Let's say we have an element that shows the text **Hello, Prateek**, where the string `Prateek` is a variable. The code would look something like this:

```
import { PolymerElement, html } from '@Polymer/Polymer/Polymer-element.js';

class HelloString extends PolymerElement {
  constructor() {
    super();
  }

  static get properties() {
    return {
      name: {
        type: String,
        value: 'No Name Provided Yet'
      }
    };
  }

  static get template() {
    return html`
      <p>Hello, [[name]]</p>
    `;
  }
}

customElements.define('hello-string', HelloString);
```

Here, the only extra thing that we are adding is the `properties` getter function. The name of the property is `name`, and the default value is `'No Name Provided Yet'`. When you are using the element, you can either simply call the element, as follows:

```
<hello-string></hello-string>
```

This would display the text **Hello, No Name Provided Yet**. Or, you can provide the name by adding an attribute like this:

```
<hello-string name="Prateek"></hello-string>
```

This would display the text **Hello, Prateek**. You can add multiple properties as well. For example, you can add `lastname` or `age` as properties as well.

But what if you have nested components and this text is a variable coming from a parent component? Let's take a look at what this code would look like:

```
import { PolymerElement, html } from '@Polymer/Polymer/Polymer-element.js';
import './hello-string.js';

class StudentName extends PolymerElement {
  constructor() {
    super();
  }

  static get properties() {
    return {
      name: {
        type: String,
        value: 'John Doe'
      }
    };
  }

  static get template() {
    return html`
      <hello-string name="[[name]]"></hello-string>
    `;
  }
}

customElements.define('student-name', StudentName);
```

Here, we are passing the `name` property as a variable to the attribute in the `<hello-string>` element. This whole process is called **data-binding**. If you would like to know more about data-binding in Polymer, you can visit the following link: `https://Polymer-library.Polymer-project.org/3.0/docs/devguide/data-binding`.

With the help of these concepts, you should be able to create Polymer elements with ease.

Stencil

Stencil is a compiler for Web Components. It uses TypeScript and JSX to create Web Components. It even comes with a lot of features that are missing in the vanilla Web Components that can be used to make good single-page web apps.

Let's get a better idea of what Stencil can do with the help of a `<hello-world>` component. This component required a little understanding of TypeScript as well as JSX. If at any point in time you would like to take a look at the docs, you can find them here:

- **TypeScript**: `https://www.typescriptlang.org/`.
- **JSX**: `https://reactjs.org/docs/introducing-jsx.html`.

I will try to keep my code as simple as possible so that you don't have to look at the docs. Now that we have that out of the way, let's create a hello-world component using Stencil.

The Hello World Stencil component

Stencil comes with a lot of features to build components. Let's first set up our folder to write a component. You can do so by typing the following command in the Terminal:

```
npm init stencil
```

You will be shown a bunch of options, from which you can select the component. On selecting the component option, feel free to enter a name for the project. I chose `stenciljs-app`. And this would print out an output that looks something like this:

```
✓   Pick a starter › component
✓   Project name › stenciljs-app
✓   All setup in 8.19 s

  Next steps:
   $ cd stenciljs-app
   $ npm start

  Further reading:
   - https://github.com/ionic-team/stencil-component-starter
```

This will create a starter project with a default component in it. You can run the project by typing the following command:

```
cd stenciljs-app
npm start
```

This will run the `stenciljs-app` project on `localhost:3333` in the browser. It will also show the default component, `<my-component>`, as a part of the output. This is technically the `<hello-world>` component provided by default inside our project. But we will create our own `<hello-world>` component from scratch.

In order to create our `<hello-world>` component, we need to first complete some pre-requisites. These are as follows:

1. Create a folder called `hello-world` inside the `src/components` folder.
2. Create a file called `hello-world.tsx` inside this `hello-world` folder. We are using the `.tsx` extension because it is a TypeScript file. Stencil will compile this file to a `.js` file. We do not have to worry about it.
3. Create another file called `hello-world.css` inside the `hello-world` folder. This is where we will be writing the CSS for this component.

Now that we have the setup complete for the `<hello-world>` component, let's start writing the code for it. This is what `hello-world.tsx` looks like:

```
import { Component, h } from '@stencil/core';

@Component({
  tag: 'hello-world',
  styleUrl: 'hello-world.css',
  shadow: true
})

export class HelloWorld {
  render() {
    return (
      <div>Hello World</div>
    );
  }
}
```

In the first line, we are importing the `Component` and `h` objects from the `stencil` library. When we talk about technical jargon, we will be calling this `@Component` as `@Component` decorator. As we can see, we are simply stating the tag for the component, the CSS it needs to use for styling, and whether the component needs to render in a shadow DOM or not. Inside the `HelloWorld` class, we are simply returning the JSX for this component. If you are from the React background, then it should be pretty straightforward. But if you are new to JSX, for the sake of simplicity, you can think of it as a way to write HTML inside JavaScript.

So, we have now created our first Stencil component. Now, to see it on the web page, you can simply add the <hello-world> tag in the index.html file inside the src directory. Stencil will pick it up automatically, create its include, and compile it for you. You just have to refresh the page.

Now that we know how to create a Stencil component, let's dive into the next section where we create nested Stencil Components.

Nested Stencil components

In the last section, we looked into the @Component decorator and how it helps create a Stencil component. In this section, we will use one more decorator called the @Prop decorator to declare the variables that will act as properties which can be passed onto other components.

Let's create an element that shows us a list of students, called <student-list>. In Stencil, it would look something like this:

```
import { Component, h } from '@stencil/core';

@Component({
  tag: 'student-list',
  styleUrl: 'student-list.css',
  shadow: true
})

export class StudentList {
  render() {
    return <div>
      <div>Student List is as follows: </div>
      <student-name class="student-list__student" first="John"
last="Doe"></student-name>
      <student-name class="student-list__student" first="Tom"
last="Hanks"></student-name>
    </div>;
  }
}
```

Here, we are doing the same thing as we have done in the <hello-world> component. We are simply importing the stencil library, then setting the name of the component and CSS styles in the @Component decorator. And, in the class, we have a component called <student-name> that has the first and last name as attributes.

Let's take a look at the definition of this `<student-name>` component:

```
import { Component, Prop, h } from '@stencil/core';

@Component({
  tag: 'student-name',
  styleUrl: 'student-name.css',
  shadow: true
})

export class StudentName {
  @Prop({reflectToAttr: true}) first: string;
  @Prop() last: string;

  private getFullName(): string {
    return `${this.first} ${this.last}`;
  }

  render() {
    return <div>Student Name: {this.getFullName()}</div>;
  }
}
```

Here, if we look inside the `StudentName` class, we can see that we are using the `@Prop` decorator. With the help of this `@Prop` decorator, we are defining two properties: `first` and `last`. The `first` property also has `reflectToAttr` set to `true`, which means that this property can be seen as an attribute when it gets called inside the `<student-list>` component:

```
▼<student-list class="hydrated" data-hmr="2109757">
  ▼#shadow-root (open)
    ▶<style s-id="sc-student-list">…</style>
    ▼<div>
        <div>Student List is as follows: </div>
      ▶<student-name class="student-list__student hydrated" first="John">…</student-name>
      ▶<student-name class="student-list__student hydrated" first="Tom">…</student-name>
    </div>
</student-list>
```

Here, we can see the attribute first in the shadow DOM for this component. But since we did not set `reflectToAttr` to `true` for the `last` property, it doesn't get reflected in the attribute.

Also, if you notice the definition of the `<student-list>` component, we did not import the `<student-name>` component. We simply started using the element. Stencil is smart enough to pick up these changes and auto-include them in the files. This way, we can create nested elements without worrying about the imports.

Now that we know how to create nested components using Stencil, let's look at one of the ways to achieve performance on to the web page we are trying to create.

Pre-rendering for Stencil components

When we talk about rending a single page web app, we are basically sending all the resources onto the page and then letting the client do all the computations to build the page. This is a computational-heavy process, which may lead to longer times to first meaningful paint on the site.

To solve this problem, Stencil comes with pre-rendering on by default. Pre-rendering lets the server generate static HTML, CSS, and JavaScript files at build time, and can then be hydrated with the data for that page. This lets users see the page faster, lets the search engine crawlers browse the site for SEO faster, and lets the user see the page even when the JavaScript is disabled on the client side.

Summary

In this chapter, we learned how to create Polymer and Stencil components. We looked into how these components can be nested to form more complex elements. We also looked into how attributes and properties can be passed into child components in both Polymer and Stencil components.

We also looked into the pre-rendering feature of Stencil, and how it can be used to make a site perform better.

In the next chapter, we will look into how vanilla Web Components can be used in various other libraries and frameworks.

8
Integrating Web Components with a Web Framework

In the previous chapters, we have either created Web Components from scratch or used a library to create Web Components. We even created a single-page web app using just Web Components. But what if we have an already-existing project? What if this is a monolithic frontend web application and we need a way to use a web component in this project? And what if we want to use a web component for a quick prototyped functionality without much overhead? This could save a lot of effort in both time and money.

This chapter is just for scenarios like this one; here we will look into ways in which we can use Web Components in already-existing projects.

 By the way, this chapter is for advanced users.

I am assuming that you have worked on React, Angular, or Vue and that you are looking for ways to include Web Components into web applications that are already using one or more of these technologies. I am also assuming that you know how to run these web applications. However, for the sake of simplicity, we will look into the simplest component that uses one of these technologies and how two Vanilla Web Components can be included in any of these technologies.

In this chapter, we're going to see the following topics:

- Integration with already-existing projects
- Integrating Web Components in React
- Integrating Web Components in Angular
- Integrating Web Components in Vue

The <header-image> web component

Let's say that we have a web component called <header-image> whose purpose is to show an image, and, on hover, it should be able to show a text that shows a small description of the image. The definition of this web component would look something like this:

```
export default class HeaderImage extends HTMLElement {
  constructor() {

    // We are not even going to touch this.
    super();

    // lets create our shadow root
    this.shadowObj = this.attachShadow({mode: 'open'});

    // Then lets render the template
    this.render();
  }

  static get observedAttributes() {
    return ['src', 'alttext'];
  }

  attributeChangedCallback(name, oldValue, newValue) {
    if (name == 'src') {
      this.src = newValue;
      this.render();
    }
    if (name == 'alttext') {
      this.alt = newValue;
      this.render();
    }
  }
  ...
  ...


}
```

As you can see, we are simply calling the super() method inside the constructor. Then we are creating a shadow root for the component and then calling the render() method. We are also making sure that any of the changes coming in via attributes re-render the web component to reflect the updates associated with these attributes.

As for the `render()` method, it looks something like the following:

```
render() {
  this.shadowObj.innerHTML = this.getTemplate();
}

getTemplate() {
  return `
    <img src="${this.getAttribute('src')}"
      alt="${this.getAttribute('alt')}"/>
    ${this.handleErrors()}
    <style>
      img {
        width: 400px;;
      }
    </style>
  `;
}
```

Here we are adding an image to the HTML of the shadow root. In addition, we are also enabling error handling with the help of the `handleErrors()` method:

```
handleErrors() {
  if(!this.getAttribute('alt')) {
    return `
      <div class="error">Missing Alt Text</div>
      <style>
        .error {
          color: red;
        }
      </style>
    `;
  }

  return ``;
}
```

This `handleErrors()` method looks for the missing attribute, `alt`, and spits out an error message asking the user to enter the `alttext`.

We can use this web component with the following HTML:

```
<header-image alttext="Blue Clouds"
src="https://www.freewebheaders.com/wordpress/wp-content/gallery/clouds-sky
/clouds-sky-header-2069-1024x300.jpg"></header-image>
```

Now that we know what our web component looks like, let's try to use it in already-existing projects. We will start with an existing project that uses React.

Integrating Web Components in React

Let's say that we have a React app. I am going to use the starter app provided by React. You are free to try this out in your more complex app. The steps for doing so are going to be exactly the same.

Setting up a React project

If you have your own app, you do not need to go through this section.

You can use the following link to set up the project: `https://facebook.github.io/create-react-app/`.

Once the setup is done, you will be left with a project that can be run using the following command:

```
npm start
```

Adding a React component

For the sake of simplicity, I am adding a React component. This React component is going to simulate a real life scenario of the component that is responsible for including the `<header-image>` web component. Let this React component be `MainBody`; its definition would look something like this:

```
import React, { Component } from 'react';

export default class MainBody extends Component {
  render() {
    return (
      <div>
        <p>This is the main body</p>
      </div>
    );
  }
}
```

As you can see, it shows just one line of text and nothing else. If you have a more complex component, the steps will be the same. As for the starter app, we will include this `MainBody` component in our `App` component first, which is shown here:

```
import React from 'react';
import logo from './logo.svg';
```

```
import './App.css';
import MainBody from './main-body/main-body.js';

function App() {
  return (
    <div className="App">
      <header className="App-header">
        <img src={logo} className="App-logo" alt="logo" />
        <p>
          Edit <code>src/App.js</code> and save to reload.
        </p>
        <a
          className="App-link"
          href="https://reactjs.org"
          target="_blank"
          rel="noopener noreferrer"
        >
          Learn React
        </a>
        <MainBody />
      </header>
    </div>
  );
}

export default App;
```

Here, we are simply importing the MainBody component and using it directly in the App component.

Integration of Vanilla Web Component in a React component

In order to use the `<header-image>` component inside the MainBody React component, we will be adding a few things to the MainBody component:

```
import React, { Component } from 'react';
import HeaderImage from '../web-components/header-image/header-image.js';

export default class MainBody extends Component {

  constructor() {
    super();
    this.state = {
      src:
```

```
'https://www.freewebheaders.com/wordpress/wp-content/gallery/clouds-sky/clo
uds-sky-header-2069-1024x300.jpg',
      altText: 'Blue Clouds'
    }
  }

  componentDidMount() {
    customElements.define('header-image', HeaderImage);
  }

  render() {
    return (
      <div>
        <p>This is the main body</p>
        <header-image alttext={this.state.altText}
          src={this.state.src}>
        </header-image>
      </div>
    );
  }
}
```

Here, we are importing our `<header-image>` web component from its respective location and then registering the custom element in the life cycle callback `componentDidMount()` method. Then, we are trying to send in `alt` and `src` via state variables to the `<header-image>` component.

The steps are the same for all the React components that are trying to use any Vanilla Web Component. Now that we have an understanding of how a web component can be used in a React project, let's take a look at how it would look inside an Angular app.

Integrating Web Components in Angular

Let's say that we have an already-existing Angular app. This could be a full-fledged project or a starter app, and we want to use the `<header-image>` web component in an Angular component. We'll start with the setup.

Setting up an Angular project

Let's say that we want to start with a starter app. We can follow the steps given at the following URL to install and serve the starter app: `https://angular.io/guide/quickstart`.

Angular does not support Vanilla Web Components by default, so even before we start using Web Components, though, we need to tell Angular that we want to use a web component. We can do so by adding the following code in the `app.module.ts` file:

```
...
import { NgModule, CUSTOM_ELEMENTS_SCHEMA } from '@angular/core';
...
...

@NgModule({
  ...
  ...
  schemas: [
   CUSTOM_ELEMENTS_SCHEMA
  ]
})
```

This is to tell Angular to expect a custom element that is not built using Angular.

Integrating with Angular

Now, let's say we have a component called `app-main-body` built using Angular (`file: main-body.component.ts`) that looks something like this:

```
import { Component, OnInit } from '@angular/core';

@Component({
  selector: 'app-main-body',
  templateUrl: './main-body.component.html',
  styleUrls: ['./main-body.component.css']
})
export class MainBodyComponent implements OnInit {
  src: string ;
  altText: string;

  constructor() {
    this.src =
'https://www.freewebheaders.com/wordpress/wp-content/gallery/clouds-sky/clo
uds-sky-header-2069-1024x300.jpg';
    this.altText = 'Blue Clouds';
```

```
    }

  ngOnInit() {
    }
  }
```

If we want to include the `<header-image>` web component here, we can simply add the following code:

```
  ...
  import HeaderImage from '../web-components/header-image/header-image.js';

  ...
  export class MainBodyComponent implements OnInit {
    ...
    ...

    ngOnInit() {
      customElements.define('header-image', HeaderImage);
    }

  }
```

Here, we are simply importing the component definition, and then inside the `ngOnInit()` callback method, we are registering the custom element. If we look at the template file, `main-body.component.html`, the web component can be included as shown in the following code:

```
<p>
  main-body works!
</p>
<header-image attr.src={{src}} attr.alttext="{{alttext}}"></header-image>
```

Here, we are passing in `src` as well as `altText` to the `<header-image>` component as attribute values. In this way, we can have Web Components built outside of Angular for use in Angular projects.

Now that we know how a Vanilla Web Component can be used in Angular projects, let's look at how Web Components can be used in Vue components.

Integrating Web Components in Vue

Vue is another one of those libraries that is growing incredibly fast, so I thought it would be a good thing if we saw how a web component can be included in a Vue component.

Let's say we have a `<main-body>` Vue component that looks something like this:

```
Vue.component('main-body', {
  props: ['src', 'alt'],
  template: `
    <p>This is the main body</p>
    `,
})
```

As you can see, it does nothing other than show text, just like the main body component in Angular and React. Let's say we want to include the `<header-image>` web component to this `<main-body>` component. This would make the `<main-body>` component look something like this:

```
import HeaderImage from '../web-components/header-image/header-image.js';

Vue.component('main-body', {
  props: ['src', 'alt'],
  template: `
    <p>This is the main body</p>
    <header-image src="{{src}}" alttext="{{alt}}"></header-image>
    `,
  created: function() {
    customElements.define('header-image', HeaderImage);
  }
})
```

Here, we are simply importing the `HeaderImage` component and registering the web component inside the `created()` callback method. As you can see, it is very simple to use a web component inside a Vue component, and the attribute values can be passed into the web component via interpolation, as shown in the previous code.

Using the process stated in this section, we can add an already-existing web component to any Vue project.

Summary

In this chapter, we looked into how we can integrate Web Components into already-existing projects that use some of the most famous libraries/frameworks in the frontend world. We learned how to add an existing web component built using Vanilla JavaScript to a React, Angular, or Vue project. The techniques learned in this chapter can be used with any framework or library and in any type of existing project. The inclusion of Web Components in already-existing projects is also a good use case for the quick prototyping of features, and the components can even be removed as soon as their work is done.

I hope that this chapter was useful in helping you create better web applications, whether they use Web Components or not.

Other Books You May Enjoy

If you enjoyed this book, you may be interested in these other books by Packt:

Learn React with TypeScript 3
Carl Rippon

ISBN: 978-1-78961-025-3

- Gain a first-hand experience of TypeScript and its productivity features
- Transpile your TypeScript code into JavaScript for it to run in a browser
- Learn relevant advanced types in TypeScript for creating strongly typed and reusable components.
- Create stateful function-based components that handle lifecycle events using hooks
- Get to know what GraphQL is and how to work with it by executing basic queries to get familiar with the syntax
- Become confident in getting good unit testing coverage on your components using Jest

Learn WebAssembly

Mike Rourke

ISBN: 978-1-78899-737-9

- Learn how WebAssembly came to be and its associated elements (text format, module, and JavaScript API)
- Create, load, and debug a WebAssembly module (editor and compiler/toolchain)
- Build a high-performance application using C and WebAssembly
- Extend WebAssembly's feature set using Emscripten by porting a game written in C++
- Explore upcoming features of WebAssembly, Node.js integration, and alternative compilation method

Leave a review - let other readers know what you think

Please share your thoughts on this book with others by leaving a review on the site that you bought it from. If you purchased the book from Amazon, please leave us an honest review on this book's Amazon page. This is vital so that other potential readers can see and use your unbiased opinion to make purchasing decisions, we can understand what our customers think about our products, and our authors can see your feedback on the title that they have worked with Packt to create. It will only take a few minutes of your time, but is valuable to other potential customers, our authors, and Packt. Thank you!

Index

www.ingramcontent.com/pod-product-compliance
Lightning Source LLC
LaVergne TN
LVHW062035060326
832903LV00062B/1680